What It's Like to be
an Airline Stewardess
FLYING
HIGH

What It's Like to be

FLYING

ELIZABETH RICH

an Airline Stewardess

HIGH

STEIN AND DAY/*Publishers*/New York

1525426

*For N.E.P., Jr.—who made this book a
reality; and for Renni Browne, my
editor and Elsie M. Rich, my mother,
who worked as hard on this book as
I did, and deserve much of the credit.*

❉

ACKNOWLEDGMENTS

I would like to thank the many friends I have made while researching this book; I could not have written it without the cooperation of the twelve major United States airlines represented in Part II:

> American
> Braniff
> Continental
> Delta
> Eastern
> National
> Northeast
> Northwest Orient
> Pan American
> Trans World
> United
> Western

I would also like to express my indebtedness to Robert Serling, the author of *Loud and Clear*, the most informative and reassuring book on air safety I have read. Much of my information and several anecdotes in the chapter on emergency training come from Mr. Serling, who loves flying as much as I do.

CONTENTS

PART II: THE AIRLINES

Choosing among airlines: qualifications,
training, uniforms, fringe benefits, union,
salary, reserve policy, travel benefits, base
cities, where to apply:

INTRODUCTION

Airline stewardesses have come a long way since the days when their training consisted of three hours of instruction in the back room of a hangar, when their operating manual totaled four mimeographed pages and their principal job was to allay the fears of male passengers.

You are about to read a book about the stewardess profession as it is in the seventies, written by a talented member of that profession. It is a book that can be read with equal enjoyment and reward by girls who are interested in becoming stewardesses, by girls who already are stewardesses, and by parents who might be worried about offspring in either of the first two categories.

It is, above all, an honest book—one that tells the stewardess story as it deserves to be told, neither sensationalized nor whitewashed. It tells the truth about a profession that has been simultaneously maligned and overglamorized. It is both entertaining and educational, because it reflects both research and personal knowledge to an enormous degree. As such, it deserves to be read by anyone with the remotest interest in aviation—if only as a welcome, badly-needed antidote for previous books on the same subject.

While Liz Rich primarily has aimed her message at future stewardesses, I hope present ones read it, too. For what I think she has accomplished is a portrayal with pride—and this, to me, is what too many stewardesses lack today. It is not entirely their fault; the demands of the jet age are largely the source of the "glorified cocktail waitress" image. But lack of pride is what is basically wrong with being a stewardess today, not only on the part of the girls themselves but in the attitude of passengers and parents alike

9

toward a career that is as much a part of commercial aviation history as the airplanes themselves. Miss Rich restores that pride, and she does it not with phony sermonizing but with advice and anecdotes and facts that crackle with sincerity, objectivity, and truth.

I hope passengers will buy this book, too. They will get a rare behind-the-scenes glimpse that could only be revealed by a girl who looks at her flying career not through rose-colored glasses but through a microscope of both fairness and affection. It abounds with humor, too—particularly when dealing with unglamorous, often hilarious circumstances in which stewardesses find themselves.

I think the greatest compliment I can pay hostess-authoress Rich is: (a) I wish I had written this book myself, and (b) if I am ever fortunate enough to have a daughter, I'm going to make her read it—so that someday I'll fulfill a lifelong ambition and pin on her wings the day she graduates from stewardess school.

ROBERT J. SERLING
Air Safety Consultant and
former aviation editor,
United Press International

AUTHOR'S FOREWORD

Some people think I have the most glamorous job in the world. Others tell me I'm just a glorified waitress. A surprised Englishman I sat next to at a dinner party gasped, "Why, I've never met one socially before," while regarding me as if I were from outer space. These are just a few of the reactions I have encountered in my career as an airline stewardess.

The glamorous image has always been wildly inaccurate. Glamour, like beauty, is in the eye of the beholder. At the other extreme are recent newspaper and magazine articles and at least one best-selling book, which suggest that the life of an airline stewardess is a sorry one indeed. After reading a few of these exposés, a girl could easily conclude that she would be mad to embark on a career that is not only underpaid and overworked, but full of more threats than a jungle—where she must deal with the constantly heightened expectations of demanding, ill-tempered passengers who not only want a drink, a meal, and tender loving care, but a strip tease as well. Such a job not only lacks glamour; it sounds downright sordid.

The airlines fume at sensational exaggerations because the image hits them where it hurts. In the next five years, United States airlines will need nearly 40,000 new stewardesses, and bad propaganda makes this monumental job of recruitment almost stupefying. Although airlines have in the past had as many as 250,000 girls in a year apply for as few as 10,000 stewardess openings, they admit that now they are forced to actively recruit girls instead of waiting for them to storm the doors.

For example, United Airlines, which employed 5000 stewardesses in 1969, expects to need 8000 by 1972. If they have been able to find only one girl in thirty suitable to train as a stewardess, they will have to lower their standards unless they have 30,000 applicants to choose from. Some airlines have already begun to ease their requirements by dropping the minimum age limit from twenty-one to nineteen, and no longer demanding a college degree or two years' working experience. And in order to avoid losing the girls they've *got,* most of the major airlines no longer require their stewardesses to quit after marrying or reaching a maximum age limit of thirty-two or thirty-five.

Why has it been so difficult for the airlines to find suitable stewardesses when they choose one trainee from as many as thirty applicants? Certainly the job requires no special skills or previous training. The answer may lie in the past discrepancy between the type of girl attracted by the prevailing image of airline stewardesses and the type of girl the companies actually want to hire. And the job itself has become a victim of airline advertising campaigns which seek to attract the male customer (about 80 percent of air passengers are men) with the glamour/sex image of his stewardess. Consequently, recruitment personnel find themselves inundated with applications from girls who think they are on the way to becoming Playmate of the Month.

Certainly, recruiters and stewardesses alike would be happier if people had a more realistic idea of the demands and the dividends of this career. It is in the interest of the airlines to create a lively competition among *well-qualified* applicants rather than lowering their standards to fill the many openings for stewardesses. The airlines are making an effort, but they need all the help they can get.

This book is an attempt to bring the career of the airline stewardess back into the realm of reality. It is not meant for the cocktail-party traveler who thinks I have a parachute stashed away in my jump seat, or for the maiden aunt who suspects that I spend my spare time on the captain's lap, or for the swingers who want to know where the action is. I hope to give an idea of how good and bad flying can be, as well as inform the prospective applicant —and anyone else who is interested—what it is really like to be a stewardess. And girls already interested in this career should find helpful advice and information to aid them in choosing the right airline.

Perhaps this book will convince many girls who have been attracted to flying for the wrong reasons or have been put off by prevalent distortions that this is a job which offers unique advantages for a not unreasonable amount of hard work.

PART I

The
Job

1

WHY IS AN INTELLIGENT GIRL LIKE YOU AN AIRLINE STEWARDESS?

The night before I set off to begin training as a stewardess, I had dinner with a man for whom I had worked at Harvard University. I announced happily that I had been hired by an airline. "Elizabeth," he said, "death before dishonor! You are an intelligent girl, how *can* you consider wasting your life batting your eyelashes and smiling at lecherous old men?" I tried to explain that the prospect of flying to Europe was much more appealing than typing his papers about Europe. But since his prejudices, like many other people's, were firmly grounded in misinformation, he concluded that I was hopelessly frivolous.

It is a popular notion that to be an airline stewardess a girl need only look reasonably attractive, keep a smile on her face, and babble away about loving people and travel. Often this isn't too far from the truth. But it does not follow that only bland, smiling girls become airline stewardesses—or, for that matter, that bland, smiling girls make the *best* stewardesses.

Still, it might appear that there is little sense in finishing high school, junior college, or college only to graduate to a job that has you running up and down the aisles of airplanes, doing mindless things like passing out meal trays and mixing drinks. And it is true that some airline recruiters seem to have mixed feelings about hiring girls who are mentally equipped to cope with a more demanding job. One stewardess I know applied to a major airline after two years of teaching Spanish to Peace Corps volunteers. Instructed to take off weight by one interviewer, and to put a little on by the next, she finally made it to her third interview in the

17

right proportions—only to have the recruiter ask, "What does an intelligent girl like you want with a job like this?"

Why indeed? There are some excellent reasons that may not be apparent to the uninitiated. Considering how many applicants the airlines have to screen before they find one suitable trainee, it is not surprising that some of them are in the process of reassessing what type of girl they want to attract. Certainly, the girl who realizes the true advantages of this career is more likely to be effective in her job. In most cases, an enlightened self-interest is a more honest and durable motivation for flying than the wide-eyed altruism some airline recruiters dream of developing a pill to induce. I have seen the burning desire to serve humanity extinguished by tears—while girls with a little more realistic perspective weather exhausting performances of the human comedy, with patience and even humor, because they appreciate the privileges flying offers them.

Perhaps the least heralded and most valuable advantage of this job is the degree of freedom it offers. It may seem paradoxical that flying—a career that requires an unusually high degree of conformity—offers more freedom and leisure to explore individual interests than any other job I know of. Quite simply, it guarantees regular financial security without the bonds of regular working hours.

A stewardess may work from twelve to eighteen days a month, flying from sixty-five to eighty-five hours. Depending on which airline she flies for, these hours may be worked on long international or transcontinental flights, or on short domestic hops that take her out in the morning and bring her home the same night. Schedules, which are arranged by the month, offer various combinations of flights: the stewardess "bids" for them according to seniority. It is seldom that she can't arrange her days off to her advantage.

All those hours to do with as she chooses. If you have ever held a nine-to-five job, even an interesting nine-to-five job, you may have felt that there never seemed to be enough time or energy left over to really pursue interests unrelated to your job. And if the nine-to-five job was particularly demanding or exciting, you probably found your free time burdened by little black clouds of worry

18

over what was likely to confront you at the office the next morning. Flying, on the other hand, is a job that you don't take home with you. Free time is truly free.

Of course, the advantage that appeals to almost any girl is travel. The desire to see the world now—not after retirement—is common to most young people; being able to afford it is not. Beginning jobs usually pay very little, and even if you earn enough to save for a trip to Europe or across the United States, a two-week vacation doesn't give you much time to travel very far or very well.

Even for college graduates, the prospects of travel or freedom from regular working hours are very limited. A girl determined to explore the possibilities in a freelance field such as writing, designing, art, or business who lacks an independent income must start at the bottom of the totem pole. And if she has a yearning for travel and adventure, she must nurture such enthusiasms with her bedtime reading eleven and a half months of the year. That is, unless she considers becoming an airline stewardess.

Free time and unique travel privileges—for an energetic and ambitious girl who wants to make the most of these opportunities, there are countless possibilities. Some girls arrange their schedules to continue studying for degrees—and there are more and more airlines willing to pay half of their employees' tuition for accredited or approved courses successfully completed. An aspiring actress can take lessons on her days off, or make the rounds of production offices and auditions. She won't starve to death while waiting for her big break—and if it never comes she can always console herself by flying to the Cannes Film Festival.

One stewardess I know is also an art dealer: on her European layovers she shops for paintings and sculpture for the American galleries she supplies. Another imports English sheep dogs, and still another, old English taxicabs. Many simply hold part-time jobs doing work they enjoy—substitute teaching, modeling, editing; volunteer work for hospitals, schools, or political parties. And airlines often enlist their stewardesses to do public relations work for them at extra pay.

Most companies will allow you to hold any additional job that doesn't conflict with your flying schedule or performance. They do reserve the right to disallow certain types of jobs (being a Playboy Bunny is out). But the general attitude seems to be approval. As the director of an airline training college told me, "If a girl does something productive with her free time, she is more likely to be a lively, interesting girl on flights."

One can, of course, overreact to the opportunities for putting spare time to good use. Very soon after I started flying, I became bored with all the time off. I took a full-time job during the week and flew to Europe on weekends—until I realized I was right back in the nine-to-five bag again, except that I was working seven days a week instead of five. I decided that there had to be a saner solution.

I then found myself a partner in a wholesale costume jewelry company, very appropriately named Maison de Fou (Nut House). I say "found myself" because my two designer partners mistook my enthusiasm for business acumen and made me vice-president and business manager. Armed with ignorance and supreme confidence, we invaded the fashion world. Our jewelry adorned the covers of several fashion magazines, and my partners earned a distinguished reputation as designers—in 1968 they were voted Designers of the Year at an industrywide jewelry competition. Finally, after three years during which their prestige rocketed while our balance sheets plummeted into the red, we went out of business.

They have since gone on to well-deserved fame and fortune as Dunn-Townsend, having shed the name of Maison de Fou and graciously accepted my resignation. We all agreed that the lunatic quality of our name and my mad approach to the checkbook were inappropriate to serious business. I learned a lot of things from those three years in the fashion world, although making money wasn't one of them. Flying gave me the opportunity to find out where my abilities did *not* lie, in this case—and kept me from having a nervous and financial breakdown over the venture. I can't describe how happy I was to go out on my flights and get away from business worries. Compared to some of our buyers, passengers were a joy to serve.

I have to add that the interest and encouragement of one of our buyers launched me on a writing career. She showed an article I had written on shopping in Paris to her husband, an editor of *Holiday,* and much to my amazement, he bought it. For me, flying complements a writing career in the best possible ways. And, thanks to Maison de Fou, I have a larger collection of costume jewelry than any other author, living or dead.

I once discussed avocations and flying with an energetic, deeply tanned stewardess who insisted that sports enthusiasts like herself get just as much out of this career as "you scholars, creative geniuses, and capitalists," as she put it. It turned out that her perennial tan was the result of playing tennis or going skiing on her days off. Under cross-examination she admitted it wasn't exactly just fun and games—she was charging eight dollars an hour for lessons, and worked very hard at being a playgirl. Still, no other job could have offered her so many opportunities for following the sun and snow as flying, with its liberal travel privileges and ample time off.

There are less energetic ways of enjoying these advantages. Two girls I flew with last year who found the New York winter depressing packed up, moved to Bermuda, and started commuting to New York twice a month to fly six-day trips. The days off between these flight assignments gave them time to enjoy a lazy life in the sun. Another friend who married an Englishman flies to New York from London for the same long trips that take her back to London on her layovers. She estimates that even considering the two hundred dollars she spends each month commuting, she still comes out ahead by a few hundred dollars. Any job she could get in London would pay her a fifth of her present salary. And the Englishman, who as her husband is accorded the same travel privileges, keeps discovering new places he wants to visit with her. It may be a long time before he allows his wife to retire.

This happy arrangement would not, of course, have been possible in the days when stewardesses were not allowed to marry. Today, thanks to union pressure and the shortage of stewardesses, airlines allow their girls to continue flying after marriage. They have discovered, to their surprise, that marriage doesn't ruin stewardesses—some even claim that it improves their work.

Flying can certainly be an ideal job for girls who want to help their husbands make ends meet. I don't know what happened to all those men who reportedly claimed they wouldn't tolerate a wife working as a stewardess, even if the airlines allowed it. I have a suspicion that they may be the same ones who are now accompanying their stewardess wives to San Francisco or London for the weekend. Or one of them might be the husband of a girl who told me in plaintive tones, "I want to have a baby, but Freddie says we have to go to Japan first. I've already been to Japan. Oh well, it'll be fun showing it to Freddie." One baby, postponed for a year. The fact is, most stewardesses' husbands show a decided reluctance to give up the life of luxury they have sampled through their wives' fringe benefits. They may never readjust to traveling less frequently, and coach class. And few girls who have enjoyed this career for its real advantages can give it up without some regrets.

Some airlines have liberalized their hiring requirements to accept divorcees, widows, and girls legally separated from their husbands, and TWA will now hire already married girls who agree to the possibility of being based away from their husbands for six months. This opens up the career to young wives whose husbands are away in the military service—offering them, as well, the prospect of visiting their husbands on leave thousands of miles away.

Northwest Orient even allows a married stewardess to take one maternity leave and then return to flying. (That unaccompanied child sitting next to you may belong to your stewardess.) A stewardess, after all, has much more time to spend with her child than the mother who works at a nine-to-five job.

Despite the growing number of flying wives, most stewardesses are still single. The average-length flying career is two years, and the airlines say they lose most of their girls to marriage. Only 6 percent quit because they are unhappy in the job. But for a larger percentage, the reason for quitting may be a combination of disenchantment with flying and the opportunity to get married.

Disenchantment usually results from one of two things: a girl has chosen this career for the wrong reason (where is all that glamour?) or she has chosen the wrong airline for her. There is a small percentage of stewardesses who quit flying and then realize that working at a nine-to-five job is not the pleasure they thought it would be. They miss the travel and freedom enough to reapply —usually to a different airline, which they choose carefully their second time around.

Boredom with travel to the same old places can produce a desire to settle down and be bored in just one place. After the first flush of excitement wears off, flying doesn't leave you that much time and energy on layover stations to be the constant tourist.

An important decision for any girl considering this career is whether she really wants to go to Europe every week or just take vacations there. In deciding, try to determine how much energy you have, and how much capacity to work long and odd hours. Some people simply can't adjust physically to the schedule of long hours of hard work along with a five- or six-hour time change. Girls who enjoy international flying can work all night, arriving in Europe after the sun has been up for hours, take a nap, get up and meet friends, go shopping, have dinner, and stay awake until midnight with little trouble. Energy and physical flexibility are going to make the difference between enjoying the best of both worlds and sleepwalking through Paris or Hong Kong.

My friends who fly domestic routes tell me I can keep my international flights and the resultant "jet lag"—they could never take the exhaustion. These girls prefer good American food, and short hops which allow them to be home at night; while I can't imagine giving up my gourmet treats or losing touch with my friends in Europe. They also like staying close enough to home to keep an eye on their men, and they are forever telling me how much nicer their passengers are. I can't see anything wrong with my passengers. though I can appreciate the domestic stewardess's fondness for the regular businessman who greets her like an old friend on his commuter flights. But then, as time goes on, I am beginning to have the same passengers again, too. The world *is* getting smaller—it just depends on how big you want to make it for yourself.

So you can see that international and domestic flying offer different advantages. Jet lag notwithstanding, the advantages of international flying may seem the most dazzling. But do keep in mind that if you don't have friends in the cities you'll be flying to, you may well enjoy working for an airline with shorter routes so that you can eventually choose to be home every night instead of in some big city where you are a stranger.

If you think you have a talent for *making* friends, you will certainly be in the right career. I mean friends, not just dates. Having a man show you a new city can be marvelous, but there will be many more flights that don't produce an eligible man than those that do. And dates may come and go—friends last. Some of the most valuable are couples who are enthusiastic about their city and want to share it with you. There is nothing more depressing than being in an unfamiliar city, eating alone, walking alone, perhaps not even understanding the language. Friends in layover cities can make the difference between really liking your job and becoming increasingly bored with it.

Whether you choose an international or a domestic airline, you should consider carefully what part of the country you want to live in. If you aren't sure of the answer to this question—that is, if like most stewardesses you come from a small town—the big airlines offer enough base cities for you to experiment with without committing yourself indefinitely. TWA, United, American, and Pan American all have bases, on both the East and West Coasts and at major cities in between. Six months is the usual length of time required before you can transfer nearer home or to another part of the country, although there are airlines with no time limit. Some girls take seasonal advantage of this mobility to follow the sun, a favorite sport, or a man.

The smaller airlines usually offer a regional choice of bases within the areas they service—Northeast, for example, flies the Eastern states and seacoast; Western services the West to Hawaii, as far up as Alaska, and down to Mexico. One advantage the smaller airlines offer is a casual, warm relationship between management and the stewardesses which generates a spirit of camaraderie that seems to be enjoyed by all. A girl working for a large airline isn't likely to know all the stewardesses at her base city, not to mention higher-ups. If being part of a closely knit group with everyone on a first-name basis is important to you, you should seriously consider a small airline. There are many to choose from.

Thanks to the amount of time off this career offers, a stewardess can gain a great deal of satisfaction in making a particular city her home. I am always amused when people unfamiliar with my job are surprised to learn that I rent an apartment by myself in

New York City. Aside from considering me mentally defective for living in New York, they invariably say that I must be wasting a great deal of money on an apartment I seldom inhabit. When I point out that I probably spend more time (about fifteen days a month) at home than they do, they are amazed. There is a distinct reluctance on the part of most people to believe that stewardesses don't live on airplanes.

Furthermore, when I'm working, I am traveling and living out of a suitcase in hotels, so my apartment is very much appreciated when I come home. It is well worth the money. It offers me solitude and rest; my own firm mattress (a relief after the spongy or lumpy substitutes provided by some hotels; my own soft pillows; my growing collection of *objets*, which lend it the appearance of a Baghdad bazaar; and most of all a quiet place where I can think, read, and write.

I have perhaps overemphasized the opportunities for dual careers and travel in flying, mainly because the portrayal of the stewardess life style in its partying, man-hunting aspects has been examined and exploited by the press and in fiction. It is true that these aspects continue to provide the prevailing image of the airline stewardess, and probably account for a majority of the fantasies which motivate thousands of young women to apply for this job each year. Certainly there are plentiful opportunities for making whoopee—more in the circumstances surrounding an airline stewardess than in most other occupations.

A stewardess's chances to meet hundreds of different people on each trip, the majority of them men, give her the edge over girls confined to an office or a school. How she meets the challenge of looking for dates or a husband in these green pastures, amidst the frustrations and demands of getting the job done, depends on her ingenuity, charm, and luck. The fact that the most approachable of these men seem to be already married—which seldom makes them feel in the least disqualified—is something she has to cope with herself. No amount of good, solid advice is going to make a girl immune to the very real charms of a married man who doesn't have her best interests at heart. My observations are merely logistical, not moral. If a girl tells me she wants to get married, and then proceeds to get involved with a man who is already married, I can't help thinking her approach is a little backward.

Some men know all the tricks, and the radar antennae other girls have for spotting the married ones were probably earned at the expense of experience. One cagey girl I know will call the personnel office of a man's company and say she's from the credit bureau, checking on his wife's application for a charge card. If they say, "What wife?" she knows she's probably safe.

For a girl not particularly obsessed with sorting out her passengers into Prince Charming and the others, there are many opportunities for meeting exciting people. It is relatively easy to strike up conversations with passengers who share or can broaden your interests. And though you may not need any brains to pour a mixed drink or pass out a meal tray, it's nice to have something upstairs when asking an intelligent question can provoke a fascinating conversation.

Passengers who enjoy their jobs and convey their enthusiasm can make a routine flight quite special. Tucked away in my memory are a snow-machine inventor, an irascible movie producer, actors, students, businessmen, and businesswomen who entertained me with good conversation and told me a lot of things I didn't know. It isn't usual to consider whether or not the passengers entertain the stewardess, but I remember these people as particularly enjoying their flights while making mine delightful.

Airborne conversations can have pleasant repercussions. A lady fashion publicist I once talked to became so excited when I told her about my jewelry company that she took me and Maison de Fou under her wing, writing a column about us and promoting our jewelry in the fashion shows her firm arranged. Another passenger, who turned out to be the chairman of the board of one of the largest transportation-leasing firms in the world, provided me with one of my most interesting layovers, in Chicago.

He mentioned that his firm had just bought some airplanes, which had to be equipped with galleys. As an expert (most stewardesses consider themselves expert on the subject), I warned him about galley design. He was so impressed that he sent a limousine for me the next morning to take me to meet the men who ran his research division.

After being shown around and having the various projects explained to me, I discovered I was not only a galley-design nut, but an industrial-design nut as well. The three of us went to lunch and, in a science-fiction mood, redesigned the entire airline industry from terminals to toilets, remedying all pet grievances. Unfortunately, I couldn't get a firm commitment from them to do research on the perfect latch for galley containers—one which would open and shut without cutting fingers or tearing nails, and whose cost I estimate at approximately two cents. I'm afraid they will continue to design burglarproof postage meters and send men to the moon while I lose my fingernails to latches.

When the fingernails go, I can always comfort myself with the thought that I may emerge from the galley to find myself serving dinner to Paul Newman. It is impossible to fly for any length of time with a major airline and not brush elbows with famous people. This is, for the most part, one of the job's advantages. Some celebrities are delightful and some of them are nasty, just like real people. Merle Oberon is charming and friendly. She once gave us a half-dozen very long stemmed roses, which caused something of a sensation at Customs. Danny Thomas entertained us for five hours straight because he can't sleep on airplanes and his wife can. Marcello Mastroiani is silent and sexy. Steve McQueen is cute and sexy. Mama Cass is nice but nervous about flying.

The fact is, celebrities, like all other passengers, come in every type you can imagine—sooner or later you are bound to have flights with people, famous or not, whom you admire or find exciting.

Some flights can be unnervingly exciting and exotic. One stewardess who had been flying routine short trips for a year was transferred to international routes. When she checked in at the gate at Kennedy for her first flight to Paris, she was astonished to find herself surrounded by heavily armed policemen, who appeared from behind chairs and doors to escort her onto the airplane. They informed her that the flight was booked by an Arabian king and his entourage, and that an anonymous phone call had warned of an assassination attempt on the king. She loved the cloak-and-dagger atmosphere and the courtly manners of the king, who presented gifts of jewelry to each stewardess at the end of the flight. International flying was glamorous and exciting beyond her fondest dreams. "The trouble is," she told me wistfully, "flying has never been the same since. I somehow can't stop expecting that all international flights will be that way. I miss the king and my police escort, and the jewelry was lovely."

Sometimes passengers, grateful and/or generous like the Arabian king, present crew members with samples of their products or promotional gifts (ranging from perfume to free passes). A friend of mine was given two passes for a grand tour of Latin America by a grateful passenger who was the president of another airline. Through his influence, she and a friend were assured VIP treatment for a memorable trip. So far, I have been given a lifetime supply of ball-point pens and a pair of gum boots.

I'm not complaining, really: a ball-point pen given to me by a celestial mechanic—they repair space capsules—saved the day for me on one flight. The pen had an aerial in one end which could be extended (and used as a pointer for celestial mechanic lectures, I suppose). The plane was very hot that day, and the flight engineer was struggling to make the cooling system work. A very pregnant woman came up to me and demanded that I make the plane cool, whereupon she sagged against a seat and began to cry. I whipped out my pen, extended the aerial, and said severely to the ball-point, "Captain, you'd better turn up the air conditioning right away. I have a passenger here who may have a baby any moment if you don't." The woman was so impressed by my quick action that she stopped crying and started imagining it was getting cooler by the second.

There is one last, obvious advantage of flying I'd like to emphasize—the spectacular visual experience if only you take the time to look out the window. With the rapid changes in perspective, take-offs and landings are constant sources of wonder—towns and cities, whether grim or beautiful, become toy settlements when set in green and brown countrysides shot through with rivers and lakes, or embraced by oceans which never seem too vast when they are broken up by the illusionary land of clouds. You see so much of the planet earth that you will never touch.

I am always overcome by a special feeling when I fly over

Greenland, with its brilliant white mountains blurring into shadows on unimaginably huge expanses of snow. As far as the eye can see there are no buildings or people to disturb their icy majesty. Such sights can have a very soothing effect on city-jangled nerves. And as for what the fleeting thought of actually *landing* down there can do for you. . . .

Whether or not the wonders of nature have the power to soothe you and make you feel pleasurably insignificant in the great scheme of things, their beauty can at least help jolt you out of a bad mood or enhance a good one.

Free time, travel, interesting people, visual splendor—an unfettered life in a larger world than other careers are likely to offer you—these are the real advantages of flying. There are certainly enough of them to appeal to a wide spectrum of girls, and there are enough types of airlines for each girl to find the one whose advantages best suit *her*.

2

I BUY ALL MY SHOES IN PARIS
and Other Fringe Benefits

The most important fringe benefit for any girl working for an airline is the inexpensive travel available when she's *not* working. Some airlines are more liberal in the regulations governing this travel than others, but even the most conservative ones make the world accessible to their employees at a reasonable price, through reduced fares, pass privileges, and other methods.

Reduced-rate fares, usually a standard agreement between all airlines, are one-quarter of the regular price on international flights; one-half on domestic flights. Depending on your airline's regulations, you may be entitled to these fares from your first day of employment or you may have to wait six months.

Pass privileges are a little more complicated to explain. Passes are actually free tickets (if you don't count the extremely small service charge involved). Depending on the airline, they may be unlimited, or restricted to as little as once-a-year use. Some airlines, like Eastern, make them available to new stewardesses upon completion of training, others after six months to a year of employment. Many airlines have reciprocal pass agreements with each other, while United has none—since its routes virtually cover the United States, it doesn't feel its employees will need to use other airlines for domestic flights. (I understand its reasoning, but I have always found that my flights on competitive airlines give me perspective on my own job.)

When using a pass or a quarter-fare reduced-rate ticket, you fly "space available." This means you have to wait until all paying passengers are boarded to determine whether or not there is a seat for you. Hardly unreasonable, but then occasionally there isn't room for you, and that can upset your plans. It isn't prudent or realistic to let yourself depend on everything going like clockwork when you are traveling space available. And you *could* end up stranded in an airport for hours or even days, if you haven't investigated the amount of traffic you're likely to encounter. You fly "space positive," not space available if you pay a 50 percent reduced rate, domestic or international.

Every airline keeps huge notebooks available to its employees with all the current information about passes and reduced rates. The notebooks will tell you such things as which airline has reciprocal pass agreements with yours, and whether or not members of your family (limited to parents and husbands) are eligible.

Once you have managed to save enough money for personal travel, deciding where to go is the only problem. To help you make the choice there is *Interline,* a magazine published strictly for airline personnel. Along with miscellaneous airline news, it gives you a list of all the current bargain tours, hotel discounts, area fares. (The airline divides its routes into areas for a set price, allowing you to visit en route all the cities it serves at no extra charge.)

For example, Alitalia is currently offering a $99 fare from the United States to sixty cities in Europe, the Near and Middle East, which even includes Moscow. For $175 you may visit the same sixty cities plus fourteen more in Africa, if you have the strength and time. These fares are space positive during the fall, winter, and spring, except in the African portion.

TWA also has area fares, the best of which is the one around the world for $199, including an excursion to East Africa. When you consider that most people have to pay more than $1500 for the same ticket, it is easy to understand the envy generated at cocktail parties when stewardesses start talking about where they are going on their next vacation.

Varig Airlines offers Latin America for a reduced fare of $99. Or, if you just want to go to Acapulco for a week, American Airlines has a pass for $16 round trip. Space-available passes on

Trans Caribbean routes are $10. That amount will also put you in Alaska for skiing via Alaska Airlines, who will help you get reduced-rate hotel and ski accommodations as well.

Current offerings like the above will surely change, but very likely in the direction of greater variety and at an even lower cost.

Sometimes small airlines in out-of-the-way places will give a pass to airline personnel who can identify themselves with an official letter. You need only give them a copy for their files. An experienced stewardess will therefore begin her travels well supplied with copies of a form letter from the company stating that she is an employee in good standing. It is hers only for the asking.

I started off on my first vacation to the Orient with more baggage than foresight, without any letters—nobody had told me I'd need them. In Hong Kong I discovered that I wasn't going to be able to fly to Saigon on my Pan Am ticket. Since my baggage was full of gifts from home for some journalist friends in Saigon, I was naturally anxious to relieve myself of this load. I spent an hour trying to convince a polite gentleman who managed the Air France office in Hong Kong to sell me a quarter-fare ticket. Finally he relented—after I had spent a few more hours in my company's office convincing them to give me a letter of identification, which they understandably felt I should have obtained before leaving.

The manager handed me my ticket and sighed when I asked him how I should make out my check. "It is much easier to give you a pass, Miss Rich." Delighted, I spent my flight to Saigon writing bouquets of compliments to Air France about its lovely Mr. Lee. He had opened a whole new world to me. I proceeded to fly to Cambodia and Bangkok on hospitable national airlines, arriving back in Hong Kong with half of my Pan Am ticket unused. Of course, Air France doesn't come under the heading of "small" airlines, and I don't want to mislead you into thinking that they give out passes like chewing gum. In this particular instance, it was my good luck in finding Mr. Lee that got me around the Far East.

Needless to say, I learned from this experience that it is better to do your footwork and paperwork at home before you begin your vacation. This is certainly true of visas. I almost had to pass up Hong Kong because I naïvely hadn't investigated the visa requirement before I left. A very kind ground hostess smuggled me in—the customs office which handled such problems was fortunately closed when I arrived in the wee hours of the morning.

Should you feel the urge to make the world a little better place to live, the airlines even provide their own mini-Peace Corps program. The Thomas Dooley Foundation works with some airlines in recruiting girls to work in Southeast Asia for three-month tours helping in hospitals, schools, and orphanages run by the foundation. The program was started in 1961 with two Pan Am volunteers who were sent to a refugee camp for Tibetan children in Darjeeling, India. Their efforts were such a success that this experiment became a program, which now includes girls from most of the major airlines.

No special skills are required, just a concern and a willingness to do whatever may be needed. Nursing or teaching experience is certainly an advantage, but most of the stewardesses who have participated just took with them the ability to work hard. Applications are submitted through your airline. If you are accepted, the airline provides round-trip transportation and a monthly subsistence allowance. The stewardesses I've talked to after their return found that the rewards of the work far outweighed the disadvantage of their temporary reduction in income.

There are also opportunities for the patriotically minded through MAC (Military Airlift Command) flights. Some airlines have contracts with the United States Government to transport troops to military bases in Southeast Asia and NATO bases in Europe. There are stewardesses who prefer to fly these MAC charters. Military personnel, especially the enlisted men, appreciate everything that is done for them on these flights. They are patient, well-behaved, good-humored, and helpful—to the point where they would do the whole job for the stewardesses if allowed. There is no liquor served on these flights, so—happy days—no drunks. It can be very refreshing to fly a MAC trip after a month of summer traffic flights carrying wall-to-wall people, all of them demanding service at the same time.

If you can weather the occasional bouts of loneliness and can bounce back to life after a few hours of sleep having stayed up all night working, there are plenty of fringe benefits for girls who fly international and transcontinental routes. For one thing, stewardesses develop very eccentric buying habits—I buy *all* my shoes in Paris—and shopping information is generously shared. Few women have any trouble assimilating this sort of material—any stewardess could more easily tell you where to buy perfume at a startling discount in Paris than where to find the Place de la Concorde. Shopkeepers know that stewardesses not only share with most of the other women in the world a weakness for fripperies and frivolities; they also carry large passenger loads of women eager for shopping tips. Many shops bring down our questionable resistance even further by giving us special stewardess discounts.

But it isn't just shops and their discounts that attract stewardesses. Girls who would never dream of carrying their own groceries home from the supermarket will fly in from Paris with a backbreaking load comprising such necessities as French bread, wine, cheese, canned goods, and butter. We have to carry our groceries, along with our suitcases, through miles of airline terminals. We drag coffee tables from the flea market in Madrid, heavy brass trays from Africa and the Middle East, rugs from Greece, pots and pans from Paris, china from London and Germany—the list could go on indefinitely. We amass loads that would make a stevedore wince, never asking ourselves the question, "Oh my God, how am I going to get this home?" until after we've paid for it. (Invariably, we know the answer: "On your back, you lunatic.") It's an incurable form of madness that goes with this career.

Sometimes I feel I'm running a food exchange between the United States and Paris. I carry Mexican food, Boston baked beans, and cake mixes to American friends living in Paris who love to see Frenchmen bite into an innocent-looking *jalapeño* pepper, or startle them with a nine-inch-high angel cake. I return with wine, cheese, snails, rare mushrooms, truffles, and spices. It's probably a blessing that Customs doesn't allow fresh vegetables or meat to be brought into the United States.

(When my partners and I were trying to publicize our jewelry company they wrote to Craig Claiborne, food editor of *The New York Times*, about my strange buying habits. Mr. Claiborne interviewed me and wrote such a flattering article that I hardly recognized myself. At a dinner party a few weeks later, I sat next to a young man who discovered from the hostess that I was that marvelous creature in Mr. Claiborne's article. He looked at me adoringly and whispered, "When I read that article, I took it to my mother and told her you were the kind of girl I wanted to marry." His devastating sincerity so rattled me that before I knew it I was telling him I couldn't even cook.)

If gourmet goodies hold no appeal for you, you can always shop for clothes that will make you the only girl you know who wears the latest fashions out of London or Paris—at least for a few months, until the fashion houses in the United States start producing their versions. (By then you're on to something else.) London is best for low-priced clothes with high style and originality. Paris is full of temptations, but has a much more detrimental effect on the checkbook. Madrid is marvelous for custom-made leather clothes; Rome, for the Pucci-Gucci crowd; the Far East for silks and custom tailoring.

Stewardesses who don't fly international routes will find that although prices don't vary greatly in American cities, their chances of finding a different style on a domestic layover are far better than if they shopped the same stores as everyone else in town. But San Francisco or Houston, London or Paris; clothes, perfume, china, or coffee tables—somehow the prospect of going shopping will usually shake a girl out of her exhaustion faster than anything else.

1525426

For theater lovers there is the joy of seeing the latest shows in London. For half the price of a Broadway show you can have the best seats in the house, and even be served tea at intermission on a silver tray. What luxury!

Stewardesses who fly the international routes never have any problem with replenishing their liquor supplies. We are allowed to bring in one bottle each trip duty free, and the prices at most international airports make it impossible to resist these bargains.

If all this doesn't excite you there are other fringe benefits to appeal to the more culturally ambitious. Many airlines offer educational aid for approved courses, and some with international routes have language laboratories which they hope will encourage their stewardesses to learn new languages or improve the foreign language they already know. Some even add the inducement of a free pass to a country on their routes where the newly learned language is used. To qualify for this pass you need only prove your proficiency by passing a very elementary language examination.

One of the most flexible aspects of flying comes under the heading "leaves of absence." The airlines have extremely liberal policies of granting time off during the seasons of low passenger loads—generally from November to March—when they find themselves overstaffed. It is possible to take from one to six months off to travel, study, or just rest. Some girls travel around for a month or two, taking advantage of passes and reduced rates to see the world as passengers for a while. Others take six months to go and live in Europe for first-hand study of the language, the literature, and the people—all those things that can be learned sitting in cafes watching the world go by.

The system creates mutual benefits. Without it, the airlines would be forced to lay off the most junior girls—who probably could not afford a surprise vacation and would therefore be the least likely to heed a call to return to their jobs one to six months later, when they were needed. You may never want to take a leave of absence, but it is an option which makes this career very attractive to some stewardesses.

The cities your airline flies to could be viewed as a fringe benefit if you have chosen the line with destinations in mind. Many girls who have traveled or studied in other parts of the world choose international airlines so they can visit cities which attract them or where they have friends. I did, and because I fly mostly to London and Paris, it sometimes works out that I see my friends in Europe more often than my friends in New York. Layovers can vary from just enough time to go to the hotel and sleep for six hours, to a week. International and transcontinental flights thus can usually be depended on to reward you with at least a day to enjoy yourself at your destination.

If you have or make friends in the cities where you have these long layovers, life can have a satisfying continuity difficult to explain to people who think stewardesses spend their layovers in hotels partying with all the other crew members or with passengers. Since I fly to London and Paris between four and six times a month, I participate to a very enjoyable degree in the lives of my friends who live there. I know through them what is going on, what people are thinking, talking about—in short, I'm not a stranger or even a visitor any more; I show up too often for that. This all makes me feel that I'm living in three great cities. Favorite destinations and friends can give roots to a flying career and dispel any feelings that you are living the life of a yo-yo, propelled aimlessly hither and yon and back again.

There are many girls (among them even some stewardesses) who firmly believe that the nicest fringe benefit of flying is the men. In my experience this is and isn't true. It is certainly true that the opportunities for meeting men are plentiful. And girls determined to find fun or a husband seldom fail. (A girl who finds neither surely can't have been determined enough.) As for the desirability and/or eligibility of the available men, the information that follows should help you judge for yourself.

First there are the crew members, of which you're bound to have at least three on every flight—captain, first officer, flight engineer. The pilots. Attractive, most of them—particularly if men in uniform, any uniform, hold a special appeal for you. Are they the ones who provide all that romance you've heard about? Well, in the first place a high percentage of the pilots are married, middle-aged men devoted to their families, the sort who wouldn't think of sweeping you off your feet. But take heart; your chances of finding an eligible crew member increase every year—lately many airlines have begun hiring new pilots.

Of course, a man doesn't have to be young and single to be attractive *and* interested in the company of stewardesses. And I suppose there is as high an incidence of stewardesses involved in an affair with the married captain as there is of secretaries who have affairs with their married bosses. The opportunity is there, and some pilots even divorce their wives to marry stewardesses, but I haven't seen it happen very often. In fact, stewardesses married to divorced pilots *or* to a new single crew member make up a very small percentage of all those I have flown with.

More often, crew members are in the category of fun, not marriage. When you are on a layover, with no plans of your own,

37

it's nice to have someone to have dinner or go sightseeing with. Even married men devoted to their families can be fun in this respect. And young or aging Lotharios (the kind who don't take this role too seriously) can be fun too. There are ample opportunities (parties, cafe-sitting, sightseeing, nightclubbing) for stewardesses to become well acquainted with the crew members. How friendly you become depends on your definition of fun. The point is, the choice is yours. You are not fated to have a mad affair with a married pilot if you become an airline stewardess, but if you want to, you can certainly find an attractive one to have it with.

Or perhaps you'd rather marry a millionaire. I know of five whole stewardesses who have. They met them in flight. Do you want to marry nobility? I know of two stewardesses who did. Movie stars, politicians, celebrities of every shape and breed— one hears of stewardesses marrying all of them. And they met them as passengers or through passengers. Doctor, lawyer, Indian chief —they are all your captive audience for the length of the flight, if you want to look at it that way.

Some girls, the kind I'd call determined, manage to find a date on every flight, but most of us meet male passengers we really want to go out with only rarely. (That isn't a complaint; I don't think I could stand one fabulous man a flight. I don't have that kind of stamina.) But those men we *have* found, whether they become friends, lovers, husbands, or pleasant memories, certainly make the job more appealing.

The important thing to remember is that most stewardesses do marry, and if you have a fixation on marrying a certain type of dream man, you are bound to meet the type sooner or later in this career. How and whether you are able to pull the dream and the reality into the conjunction of matrimony depends, as I said, on determination. It may not be very likely if your demands are highly specific, but it is always possible.

Perhaps the most significant fringe benefit of flying is that almost anything *is* possible. You can never tell what the next flight will bring. It is a delicious unknown if you're an optimist.

3

SOMETIMES EVERYWHERE IS NOWHERE

Now that you are aware of the advantages and fringe benefits of flying, you had better consider the disadvantages. While flying does away with being tied to the desk from nine to five, it presents the danger of leading a completely aimless life. Instead of being ridiculously fettered, it is ridiculously free. Unprogrammed time *can* be a curse—a few girls find it so boring or unsettling that they gladly quit for a job with regular hours.

The most aggravating aspect of the free time is that it isn't always where you might want it to be—for instance, four hours in an airport in Cleveland, while you sit and wait for your return flight, or twelve hours in the terminal in Munich while you wait for an engine to be changed, or a layover in some sleepy town where you don't know anyone.

How you react to such free time in a relatively confined area can determine your whole attitude toward the job. If you're the kind of girl who can always find *something* to do—even if it's just reading or working a crossword puzzle—you'll be fine. If you get unhappy when left to your own devices, you might hate it. I once flew with a girl who seemed to spend all her spare time applying make-up, experimenting away for hours at a time. This may be a freaky extreme, but self-absorption is better than no absorption at all. At least you don't have to resort to cleaning out your desk in order to look busy.

All too often, a stewardess's response to free time on and off the job is a desire to sleep. On some flights I have had the distinct impression that I work with a bunch of somnambulists. And people who spend all their time sleeping aren't exactly the liveliest companions; when they aren't sleeping, you can guess the topic of conversation—how tired they are.

Thanks to the irregular hours, time changes, and unexpected delays, there is a very genuine exhaustion to deal with in this job. Physical resiliency is therefore an absolute necessity for enjoyment of flying. Most healthy young women can adjust to the shifting physical demands without much effort. It is the psychological adjustment that usually seems to be the hitch.

One of the effects of exhaustion for some stewardesses is a constant battle with colds. The temperature of airplanes sometimes fluctuates from too cold to too hot. You *are* roasting as you run around or stand in front of a hot oven; the passengers must be kept warm because they're sitting still—sometimes. Or the plane's heating system isn't working too well, and everyone but the busy stewardesses is bundled up in a blanket.

I finally ended my own tendency to provide permanent residence for cold germs by taking the advice of a flight engineer who claimed that large doses of vitamin C kept him from catching colds. As every doctor I asked told me this was ridiculous, I ignored his advice for about two years—until, after another winter and summer of sneezing, I tried vitamin C in desperation. Magic: no more colds, or at least almost no more colds. Certainly a vast improvement over my former condition. It may be ridiculous, Doctor, but I don't care whether my resistance is mental or physical; vitamin C works for me.

There is one psychological-physical adjustment I don't think I'll ever succeed in making. If I fly to Europe and have an intermediate stop before reaching my layover destination, I know I'm going to have troubles. Picture yourself working all night long for seven hours. By the time you land at, say, London, your bones ache, your legs ache, and most of all your eyeballs ache. After bidding all your sleepy passengers goodbye in London, you welcome a whole new set of passengers on their way to Frankfurt. They, having just gotten up from a good night's sleep, board the flight bright and cheerful, assuming you feel the same way they do. It is a terrible shock to the system.

I sometimes have fantasies about capturing the scheduling

committees who dream up those trips for us and making *them* work one. I would rather work a fifteen-hour trip, nonstop—at least the passengers run down at about the same rate you do. Some even say soothing things like, "I don't know how you girls do it, you must be exhausted." They *appreciate* the dopey smile they get with their sweet roll and coffee instead of wondering if the airlines have started hiring the mentally retarded.

The point is, there is very little a stewardess can do about the fateful hand of the scheduler, or the increasing work loads the company dreams up to lure more passengers or cut costs. When I began flying, every international flight had six stewardesses and one purser, or male steward. A few years later, as part of a big cost-cutting campaign, the airlines decided the job could be done with one less girl. We all moaned, but we did the job so well that, after a year, it was decided to remove yet another girl on those flights not carrying a certain percentage of passengers.

We now manage with four girls and one purser, sometimes even with full loads when the extra girl isn't available. But I very much miss the fun and flourish of the good old days. It is simply a matter of economics to the airlines; I suppose their reasoning would be that they are not paying us to have fun, and flourish doesn't attract more passengers. Bitter arguments on this subject still take place between unions and management, never to be resolved, I suppose. We just grit our teeth when passengers tell us Japan Air Lines has nine people to do the same job we're doing.

Those good old days very often used to include layovers in Europe that gave you two- and three-day holidays at the company's expense. Now, most European layovers are a day and a half at the most. There's a reason why the longer ones are rare these days; flights to Europe have increased so much that there's usually a return flight for crews to work the next day. Again, a matter of economics, and one more fringe benefit done away with. My reminiscences of three lovely days in Athens or Rome are greeted by new girls with the same amused tolerance I used to give very senior girls talking about the week-long European layovers in the days of the propeller. You can't miss a benefit you've never enjoyed.

The unions, of course, will often fight change in the course of protecting stewardesses' interests, but too often they lose. As for the stewardesses, they're expected to be ever adjustable to change, to go on and smile, and woo the passengers to come back and fly with them again. Those of us who like this job in spite of unpleasant surprises manage.

The most unpleasant surprises are usually suffered by new stewardesses, whose enthusiasm and excitement at being able to fly at all makes them better able to withstand the insecurities they will surely suffer at the hands of Scheduling. During training they have learned words and phrases like "scheduling," "holding a flight," "bidding," and "reserve." The real meaning of all those words for new stewardesses is: low man on the totem pole.

"Scheduling" assigns the flights and bids to stewardesses. "Bids" are monthly sequences of flights which let a girl know when she will be away and when she will be home, where she is going, and what her flight time for the month will be. Bids are awarded according to seniority. Every base city has more stewardesses than are needed to man the flights they operate. Those junior girls who can't "hold a bid" make up the "reserves" or the "pool." Reserve stewardesses are called out to work unexpected charter flights or, more likely, the flights of girls who are sick or off duty. Since a stewardess never calls in sick until the day of her flight, reserves seldom know where they are going until the day they go.

While on reserve, you are instructed to stay in your apartment and wait patiently until you are called. You are assigned a certain number of days off a month; the rest, you spend near the telephone. You can't even wash your hair or go to the post office without asking permission from Scheduling.

Scheduling invariably calls while you are setting a gourmet dinner for two on the candlelit table, and tells you to be at the airport in an hour. Just as perversely, they can be counted on *not* to call at any point during the weekend you could have gone skiing.

It sounds grim, and it can be—reserve is an awful sort of limbo. But as is the case with most depressing situations, there are ways of making the best of it.

If you get called out on more than your share of flights during the month, you will surely be exhausted by the end of it. But then, you will surely be able to drag yourself to the bank and deposit all that expense money and overtime pay. Much worse is not being called, or being called only once or twice during the month. Spending that amount of time inside your apartment, you can go broke and crazy at the same time.

Even this fate can be avoided, fortunately, no matter how slow the month. When I graduated from training I was based in San Francisco, which had such popular flights and such healthy stewardesses that I was averaging one flight every eight to ten days. After a few weeks of enjoying my leisure, I began to feel the walls closing in around me. When I received my first meager paycheck and even tinier expense check, I decided it was time for action. Having caught on to the system of calling Scheduling to find out my number on the reserve list—if they told me I was number twenty-four, I could be fairly sure I wasn't going out that day—I found a part-time job. I'd then call in, ask if I could go out for an hour, take my uniform to the office, call Scheduling again and leave a new call number, work all day, and repeat the phone calls when I went home in the evening. I thus relieved myself of boredom and financial problems at the same time. You'd be surprised at how many jobs are open on this hit-or-miss basis. Finding them may take a little shopping around, but they do exist.

Overall, Scheduling's fickle finger of fate has been very kind to me in the job, but there are others who haven't fared so well. I'm glad I wasn't among the girls who had been holding flights for two years and were bumped back to reserve after airlines removed a girl in their economy drive. It's a nasty shock to suddenly be denied a privilege you feel you have earned and consequently take for granted. And I'd hate to have been the frantic stewardess who discovered she was being taken from her Chicago base to work out of New York—two weeks before her wedding. They can't do that to you? They can and do. If stewardesses are needed at a base and not enough volunteers come forward, the most junior girls are drafted. Be assured it is a rare occurrence, but forewarned is forearmed. And remember you said you loved to travel.

"Temporary assignments" are another threat to a stewardess's sanity. They promise a shade more insecurity than just being drafted from your base for a stated period of time. Here's how they work: You are on reserve. You are informed that you will be sent to, say, New York from your base in San Francisco. For how long? you ask. Until you are no longer needed in New York, silly. You leave San Francisco unenlightened about your future. You are installed in a hotel, where you remain on call in the same old reserve manner. You go out on trips and stay in hotels and then come back to a hotel. That kind of life can drive you quite mad in no time at all.

It happened to one of my roommates in San Francisco. She was miserable at the thought of working out of New York—and I, homesick, envied her the assignment—could we swap? The answer was no, and after weeks of hotel living without one flight home to San Francisco, she quit.

Situations like these can easily give you a persecution complex, especially if you find it only reasonable that special consideration be given you for the human frailty of wanting some guaranteed security. The fact is, you are just one stewardess in thousands to the company, which has neither the time, facilities, nor money to nurse ailing psyches.

The hotels provided by your company at layover destinations are another source of joy and despair. Some, although not many, are great. More often they are mediocre to bad. It is very depressing to walk into a hotel room after a long, hard trip and find unemptied ashtrays or dirty bathrooms. It is even worse to find that your room hasn't yet been vacated. All you want to do is crawl into bed: so sorry, your room won't be ready for two hours. Depending on how tired you are, your response may vary from grim resignation to thoughts of suicide.

Hotels are a big problem for the airlines. They try to make long contractual arrangements to ensure rooms for crew, but what if a flight is canceled while a big convention is in town? Naturally, the hotel will feel safe in letting the rooms to other guests. If you do show up ("Surprise, we didn't cancel after all, we're only eight hours late"), and Scheduling didn't call the hotel to let them know, it's hours before you are finally bedded down for the night.

One of the most maddening solutions the airlines find to problems like this is to put stewardesses up at the airport motel. For short layovers, following an exhausting flight, this is fine—you're too bleary-eyed to care if the bed is on the end of the runway. But for long layovers, it is not my idea of relaxation to watch airplanes land and take off. And most airports are such a distance from the cities that it is both time-consuming and expensive to venture into town for a few hours. Unions try to keep this practice to a minimum, but it happens.

If you have strong feelings about being home for the holidays, please be warned that new stewardesses are those angels who fly everyone else home for Christmas and Thanksgiving. You could be lucky and discover that your layover destination is also your home town, but the chances against that are probably a million to one.

My first Christmas flying was spent in Indianapolis at a grim hotel whose personnel were totally lacking in holiday cheer. Neither my flying partner nor I knew anybody for miles around. The only bright note in the whole ghastly layover was a midnight phone call from a passenger who had deplaned at Cleveland. Having noticed our expressions when he told us how happy he was to be joining his family for Christmas, he was now calling to tell us that he hoped next year we would really have a merry Christmas.

That did it. We had managed to be fairly stoical about our fate before his call, but now we both got sniffly as we took turns thanking him—while *he* became more and more distressed at having upset us. We hiccupped good-bye, assuring him we were touched, and crying only from happiness. We cried, in fact, until we had to laugh at the piteous scene we were enacting. Merry Christmas!

When the next Christmas rolled around, my prospects looked better. I had a flight back from Paris on Christmas Eve. My mother was going to wait for me in my apartment, whereupon we would both take a train to Philadelphia and join the family celebrations. Delighted with my luck, I was ill prepared for another surprise: when Scheduling doesn't get you, the weather will. The forecasts during the flight from Paris became more and more dismal. The whole Eastern Seaboard was smothering under a blizzard—no chance of landing anywhere near New York.

To add to the nightmare, there were a dozen or so Greek-speaking passengers who had no idea of a change in destination.

As none of us happened to speak Greek, we tried to show them with maps that we would be landing in Montreal instead of New York. This tactic only seemed to bewilder them, so we put our arms out like airplanes and swooped down on the map to Montreal. Hilarity reigned—they being convinced, I'm sure, that we were insane. As it turned out, no less than twenty-three unexpected airplanes had arrived at the Montreal airport and deposited a few thousand forlorn and tearful passengers: the place looked like a refugee camp. The Greeks at last realized that they weren't in New York, panic being narrowly averted by a Greek-speaking agent who gently explained the situation to them. There was no possibility of unloading the baggage on all those airplanes, so we were herded into a bus and taken to a motel—which was a blessing because many passengers never found a bed that Christmas Eve. Phone lines were tied up for six or seven hours, and drugstores ran out of toothbrushes. (Note: *Always* carry a toothbrush in your handbag.) The next morning being bright and sunny, we flew back to a New York decked out in a blanket of white. I arrived at my empty apartment, muttered, "To hell with holidays," and went to bed. Merry Christmas!

One cheering thought; there will always be another Christmas, and seniority increases your chances of actually having a merry one.

So there you are, a victim of Scheduling and the weather. But with a bit of luck and seniority you can avoid becoming paranoid and actually enjoy your job—*if* you learn to cope with difficult passengers, who have to be classified as a real disadvantage of flying.

Most passengers are pleasant or at least polite, a few are exciting and fascinating, and some are rotten to the core. You are, after all, working with a cross section of humanity. I offer here a few basic psychological facts which may help you understand why some of your flights suddenly resemble the inside of a nursery school or, on rare occasions, a lunatic asylum.

Even in this jet age of ours, flying is a terrifying experience for many passengers. In threatening situations, people tend to revert to childhood. If they were well-behaved, secure children, then they are likely to be quiet, polite passengers who—despite their fear of crashing and burning any minute—sit numbly waiting for it all to be over. But then you have the other kind who were undoubtedly little monsters until they grew up to be big monsters. They distract themselves by demanding impossible service, making scenes, or even throwing tantrums. The only way for them to relieve the torture of flying is to torture you.

The temptation to be knowledgeably condescending to such a passenger should be resisted; it only provokes a worse situation. There is no hope of making them see reason, because they are temporarily insane. The best course is to steer clear of them. If that is impossible, just concentrate on what rotten children they must have been when they tell *you* what a stupid, worthless, incompetent you are because the company doesn't carry their brand of scotch. If you take any of these attacks personally, you are lost. Just pray the passenger means it when he threatens never to fly your airline again.

It took only one hair-raising experience to keep me from ever attempting to put one of these bullies in his place. I was working a late flight from New York to Chicago, with an intermediate stop in Washington, D.C. The last passenger to board there was unshaven and obviously drunk. There was something so menacing about this man that after taking one look at him I decided I wasn't going near him. He sat down and proceeded to drink furtively from a bottle he was hiding under his coat. This is illegal, and I considered confiscating his bottle until the end of the flight. My flying partner and I talked it over and decided to ignore the situation—the scene he might make would certainly disturb other passengers.

At one point the man sitting next to him came back to us and asked if he could sit and talk with us: the Menace was bothering him. We apologized and asked him please to take another seat. Fortunately he was agreeable, but he alarmed us even more by saying, "I'm a doctor and I'd be willing to bet that guy is not only drunk but crazy. He talked to me for about fifteen minutes and I couldn't make any sense out of what he said." With the doctor gone, the man proceeded to hang his legs over the arm of his seat and kick the seat across the aisle, waking up a young girl. Before we could decide what to do about that, the girl got up and came back, so we asked *her* to take another seat.

Before long the man was surrounded by empty seats, and to our great relief he finally passed out or went to sleep. He lurched off the plane in Chicago and we forgot about him. The next week, on our way through Washington, a man got on the plane, flashed an FBI card at us, and asked us to come into the terminal. One at a time we were taken into a room with police and other FBI agents and seated at a table covered with mug shots. One of them asked me if I recognized any of the men in the pictures. None of them looked familiar. Finally he picked up a photograph and said, "What about this one? Do you remember him on your flight last week?" Still, no recognition. "He was drunk when he boarded the flight."

I had momentary heart failure. "That's not the scrawny little guy who gave us so much trouble? This man looks well-fed and about six feet tall. What did he do?" He turned the picture over and read me the vital statistics: height five feet five, weight 130. "That's the one, all right. And you're lucky he didn't give you any more trouble than he did. He's on the ten most wanted list—robbed a bank and killed a policeman before he boarded your flight. He was carrying a bag with the stolen money and five loaded guns."

I nearly fainted. Scenes kept flashing through my mind of me in a different mood, trying to confiscate his liquor bottle—bang, you're dead—telling him to stop bothering the other passengers—bang, you're dead—bringing the captain back to impress him into behaving with authority—bang, the captain is dead. Bang, bang, bang, all five guns going at once.

"It's sure a good thing you didn't try to touch his ditty bag," one of the policemen said helpfully, and added yet another nightmare scene to the roundup already galloping through my mind. I finally got a grip on myself and banished these ghastly visions. "Have you caught him yet?" No, they hadn't caught him but they assured me that they knew where he was. I was too rattled to ask why, if they knew where he was, they hadn't arrested him. Probably because they couldn't recognize him from the mug shot. They gave me a phone number and told me to call if I remembered anything more about the man. I went back to the airplane in a daze, with an occasional bang, bang echoing in my mind—and a firm resolve to let troublemakers alone whenever possible.

Passenger agents, like stewardesses, often develop a hands-off attitude toward obstreperous people. But I know of one agent who devised a brilliant tactic for relieving a stewardess of a very drunk and offensive passenger. The passenger was already making an unpleasant scene, even before the plane's doors were closed, and so the stewardess asked the agent to take him off the flight. The agent went up to the man and said very quietly, "If you don't settle down, sir, the plane can't take off for Montreal." "Montreal," roared the man; "I want to go to Boston," and stumbled out the door. The plane then took off for Boston.

Most stewardesses develop various maneuvers to avoid confrontations with difficult passengers, but there are always those few occasions when your patience runs out. I once witnessed a scene in which a resourceful stewardess won hands down—a rare occurrence. It was on a nonstop flight from Athens to New York with not one empty seat. This ordinarily long flight was made even longer by a delay in landing; everyone was queasy and ill-tempered from circling over New York. We had run out of nearly all of our supplies when a passenger stopped a pretty redheaded stewardess and demanded a cup of tea. She said very politely that there was no more tea; could she offer him coffee or a soft drink? "This is outrageous," he stormed. "BOAC has tea, Pan American has tea, who ever heard of running out of tea? You are all incompetent, this is the worst service I've ever had." The stewardess calmly asked if she might explain the situation.

"Before we boarded this flight," she said, "the captain told us it would be very full and very long, and that Commissary had boarded all the supplies we had room for. He also told us we had a decision to make—whether we should board one more case of tea bags or take you. I voted to take you." The other passengers, who had followed her elaborate explanation with great amusement, applauded when she finished. The man couldn't believe he had seriously given his attention to this devastating put-down. What was worse, his feeble reply was drowned out by the clapping.

Deflated but not defused, he later wrote a letter to the company demanding that the stewardess be fired for her rudeness and threatening never to fly with the airline again. Fortunately for her, four passengers from the cheering section also wrote in, commending the stewardess for her wit and promising never to fly any other airline if they could help it. The stewardess' office was then faced with the dilemma of reprimanding and commending this girl at the same time. They eventually let her off with the mild admonishment to curb her sense of humor because some people don't appreciate wit.

This story is a good illustration of what some stewardesses call the orchids-onions system. If you get a bad letter from a passenger—an onion—as far as the company is concerned you're guilty. They can't and don't take the time to find out if, perhaps, the passenger isn't some kind of nut. Depending on your former record and the seriousness of the charge, your sentence can range from a light reprimand to dismissal. But if you get an orchid letter from someone on the same flight, your supervisor (once a stewardess herself) will probably just ask you to explain without accusing you of sabotaging the company's public relations. Your orchid letter is your witness for the defense, and you have a good chance to convince her that the author of the onion letter was impossibly demanding. It is therefore a good idea to make sure you find a nice passenger to write you an orchid letter when a difficult one threatens to have you fired. It's best to assume he means it.

And what about the lecherous old, young, middle-aged men who are constantly pinching, propositioning, and generally making life miserable for the poor airline stewardess? Some books and articles would have you believe that every flight holds some kind of pervert just waiting for the moment to accost you. My first impulse is to laugh when people bring up this subject. An informal survey I have taken shows that I am more likely to be pinched in the subway than in an airplane. I can't deny that it must happen occasionally, but it hasn't happened to me or to any of the girls I've flown with.

I have had my share of the more common type of passenger— the man who fancies himself irresistible and, *if* you give him the chance, will with elephantine grace say something like, "Hey, honey, how about you and me having a few snorts together tonight, ha, ha. You stews really know how to swing." Often he is that great American classic, the traveling salesman. It's my opinion that if one of these poetic invitations were actually to be accepted, this type of man might fall apart in astonishment. But if you decline politely—and change the subject—*some* of them can be enjoyable raconteurs.

All these situations have to be played by ear. You can spot the lecherous type a mile away, and it's easy to get away if you suspect one of them is going to get offensive. You just say you have work to do and disappear for a while into the cockpit or the next cabin.

Learning to handle these situations is sometimes difficult for younger girls who have led fairly sheltered lives. I remember one flight when a loud, fat man was getting roaring drunk in the lounge. He kept shouting for me to come over, and I kept telling him I was busy and that I could hear him from the galley. Ten horses couldn't have dragged me within arm's length of that man. Unfortunately, a very young stewardess came up from the back of the airplane and heeded his call before I could catch her. He grabbed her and pulled her into his lap, and she burst into tears. It took me an hour to calm her down.

That is the only time I have ever seen a stewardess physically assaulted on the airplane, and I can't describe it as very serious. It was unpleasant, yes, but the girl admitted afterward that it was partly her own fault. You just don't walk wide-eyed into the arms of a raucously drunk man.

A flying career assures other, minor aggravations which may seem serious handicaps to the girl expecting glamour. Having been given instructions on make-up and hair styling and issued a brand-new uniform, you are told that your bandbox appearance and friendly manner are the company's main assets. You work your first flight, sincerely intending to maintain all these high standards —and find that it is difficult to look glamorous while surrounded by garbage. You soon stop asking where all of it comes from and begin to wonder where it is supposed to *go*.

Surrounded by overflowing trash bins and splitting refuse

bags, you think: Ah, glorified waitress, glorified sanitation worker is more like it. And while you are juggling empty juice cans, a passenger will offer you a dirty paper cup which, when you hurriedly compress it to save a little space and time, squirts unknown liquids at your hair, make-up, or uniform. Then there are the detestable little cream containers that explode like baby bombs when they fall off the trays, covering your legs and filling the crevices of your shoes—which does not improve their smell when the cream sours and dries. You've torn your nails on a latch, burned your fingers on the ovens, and run your stockings on a metal carrier. It's time to climb out of the garbage and repair your deteriorating appearance so you can dazzle the passengers with your glamorous image. Some of us manage, with varying degrees of success.

I often wonder why a trash eater hasn't been developed to compress all that garbage. The only one in operation now is *feet:* cover the bin with newspaper and jump on it. But you wouldn't want to take any power from the vital functioning parts of the airplane to operate a trash eater, would you? Well, no, when faced with such a choice, safety is more important than solving the garbage problem. The majority of the money spent on design-ing airplanes is rightly used to make sure they fly safely. The in-teriors are often where the costs are cut—to be specific, the galleys.

I had a taste of the difficulties management has to deal with when I was sent to look at a mock-up of one of the new jumbo jets. The director of our dining has been a passenger on one of my flights, and I had used the opportunity to point out a few of my grievances. He turned out to be an intelligent, concerned, and agreeable man, not the perverse ogre I had imagined anyone con-nected with the design of airplane galleys to be. Instead of telling me about his problems, as he well might have, he listened sym-pathetically and invited me to come into the office for a month to help the company avoid making the same mistakes in the galley designs of the new airplanes.

After thirty days of visiting commissaries (the places which prepare meals and check the equipment to service the flights) and airplane manufacturing companies, my mind was overfull of the myriad details to be considered in designing a galley, the cost and weight restrictions which influence every decision to be made. I also realized that my quarrel wasn't with my airline but with the aircraft and galley equipment companies the airlines contract to design this equipment. Some of them employ ex-stewardesses, whom they consult on galley design, which struck me as sensible. But too many don't make the connection that they could save themselves and the airlines a lot of money and stewardesses a lot of frustration *and* injury, if they had a standard policy of consulting working stewardesses about the practicality of new equipment.

But then, maybe even that wouldn't help. I once made a suggestion for a new galley drain which my airline thought worthy enough to give to a galley equipment firm for design and manufacture. When it was installed, I discovered to my horror that the designer's interpretation of my suggestion was even worse than the existing drain. To add insult to injury I had to defend myself from the accusations of other stewardesses who thought of me as that idiot who designed this monstrosity. I wrote an angry letter to the company, pointing out that although water no longer backed up out of the sink into the galley, the new drain had a lip so high that it was impossible to insert and fill a water pitcher—one of its main functions. I also suggested that they might at least have let me examine it before promoting it with my name.

Thanks to a flood of complaints, the order for the drain was canceled and the galley equipment company was left with five thousand dollars' worth of useless drains on their hands. All this expense and bother could have been avoided if the designers had consulted stewardesses *before* going ahead with manufacture.

While working in the airline's main office I began to see the insidious network of controls and pressures which frustrate the people dedicated to running the airline smoothly and making everyone happy. I gained increasing respect for the way the man I was working for coped with the never-ending problems and demands. I gratefully went back to flying at the end of the month and started trying to apply a little patience (with not very much success) when I encounter stupid designs. Undaunted, I still write suggestions, which oddly enough haven't been met with much receptiveness since the drain fiasco.

I have time to dream up suggestions for my company because

the purser on international flights makes out most of the forms and control sheets—the job of the stewardess on domestic flights. It can be a time-consuming and exacting task; if you're tired and make a wrong liquor count, you have to make up the discrepancy in revenue out of your pocket. The larger airlines become, the more paperwork in quintuplicate seems to be demanded. Every department is checking on every other, and the files overflow with all those reassuring reports fed into computers—which surely must be getting indigestion from them.

Add to the minor irritation of paperwork the heavy hand of advertising agencies whose fantasies about stewardesses are often translated into campaigns which turn into exasperating jokes at our expense. In the past, the emphasis has too seldom been on service or on the fact that flying is *supposed* to be faster; instead, the public is regularly confronted with the implication that love or sex is the airlines' main commodity—illustrated by old airline ad campaign slogans such as "Love at First Flight" and "The Air Strip." Climb out of that garbage and tell me, "When does love begin?"

To the credit of the general public, they don't usually believe all this nonsense, but stewardesses will have to laugh politely at the same old jokes for years to come.

If you have found all the disadvantages in this chapter too discouraging, let me assure you that those of us who enjoy flying in spite of them are seldom overwhelmed by the disadvantages. You should know about them, but you should also realize that the majority of the time you are not their victim—and if you know how to handle certain problems, you needn't be bothered by them at all.

The unstartling truth is that you can't have a great degree of freedom without paying for it with some degree of conformity and routine. In a flying career, the periods of freedom are in sharpest contrast to the periods of conformity. It is up to you to decide whether or not this appeals to you more than the regular intermingling of these two unavoidable aspects of life that is offered by other jobs. I can say only that most stewardesses, well aware of the disadvantages, would rather fly than not.

4

WANTED: AN OCTOPUS ON ROLLER SKATES SHAPED LIKE RAQUEL WELCH

If having read this far you are reasonably sure you'd enjoy being a stewardess, you should now learn what it takes to be one—and whether you've *got* what it takes. If you believe everything you read about stewardesses, you might think the only creature who could successfully perform the tasks and conform to the image would be the fabulous creature described in the title of this chapter. Were someone to produce such a transmutation, the airlines would be the first to weep with joy. Until then, they will have to be satisfied with hiring healthy young women whose (two) hands and feet move, and whose shape is satisfactory.

If you still think you want to be a stewardess, you were probably more amused than disturbed by the previous chapter. That is a very good sign, because flying definitely requires a sense of humor. This career can accommodate a wide range of personalities and eccentricities, but there are a few other basic qualities on which you had better have a firm grip, or you will be very unhappy —specifically: adjustability, energy, tolerance, and self-control. I am assuming, but I had better say it anyway, that you wouldn't be attracted to this career in the first place if you actively hated 99.9 percent of humanity or were allergic to strenuous physical work. Let me discourage any misanthropes or hothouse flowers from the misconception that they might be able to coast into this job just to enjoy its advantages and fringe benefits. You have to work not only with passengers but with the rest of us, and any stewardess who makes our job harder by acting like a passenger isn't tolerated very long.

I mentioned earlier that an enlightened self-interest is more valid motivation to be a stewardess than a burning desire to serve humanity. I want to add that a combination of both would be ideal, but is, in my experience, virtually nonexistent. In fact, the only girl I know who would fit into such a category would be amazed if I described her in this way. All of Margaret's qualities which come under the heading of "desire to serve humanity" are completely unself-conscious. She is just naturally patient, helpful, tolerant, and thoughtful. Combine these attributes with intelligence and a knack for organization, and you are approaching perfection. In addition, her rather lovely face seems to have a magically calming effect on the most difficult passengers.

Margaret would be positively unreal and sickening if she didn't season all this with a wry sense of humor. When I fly with her I sometimes wonder if she *ever* loses her patience or has days when she falls apart like the rest of us. I have seen her in the most trying circumstances, and she's never cracked. I remember one crowded flight when she was a passenger and we were all going quietly mad: she actually came back and worked the galley for the whole meal service, enabling us to get the trays off the other passengers' laps before the plane landed.

Lacking a few of Margaret's sterling qualities, you can still get along fine in this job. Lacking all of them, you will be a disaster. Flying can be a near paradise for two very different types of girls, and something else to those who fall in between. To risk generalizing these two types: the first is the fairly uncomplicated, outgoing, good-natured girl who is content so long as she has someone to talk to and can keep moving. She is usually looking for a husband and probably has never had any trouble getting dates. She lives with roommates not unlike her, and they keep each other entertained, spending a lot of time going to and giving parties. When she is flying, she is competent and hard-working as well as pleasant to work *with*.

Boredom isn't really a problem for this type of girl because she is seldom alone and not prone to introspection. If there is a dull period, she has the perfect solution offered by her travel privileges and flies off to Puerto Rico or Las Vegas for a few days. This girl will marry and have children after one or two years of enjoying her career, and her chances for success in matrimony are reportedly extremely good. The national divorce rate is one out of every four marriages; the divorce rate for stewardesses is one out of every forty-seven marriages.

The airlines, proud of these statistics, attribute them to the girls' training in their jobs. But the type of girl I'm talking about more likely just had the good sense to know that a few years of flying would satisfy any restlessness and vent her high spirits, preparing her to settle down happily when the fun began to be repetitious. Still, to give the airlines some of the credit, a stewardess does have to deal with every type of man and mood, learn to be calm in the face of chaos and crisis, and take a great deal of responsibility for which she is seldom recognized. All this experience, plus her finesse at being a gracious hostess, is sure to be called upon in marriage. Some men obviously consider it more valuable than a dowry.

The second type of girl is a little more difficult to generalize about. Perhaps stewardesses in this category could best be called "gypsy eccentrics." By "gypsy" I mean to imply a continuing satisfaction with the travel offered by a flying career, not just a satiation with restlessness. "Eccentric" is used with the respect that the English pay it, and the English love and nurture their eccentrics. This type of girl upsets the general conception of the airline stewardess, usually the first type.

I have already given quite a few examples of stewardesses possibly eccentric, whose avocations suggest some of the imaginative ways in which the advantages of flying can be used. And one of the common bonds among all stewardesses being an enjoyment of travel, some of them find they appreciate the travel and freedom too much to want to settle down after the customary two years. A few never settle down at all. I know a stewardess who has flown for over thirty years and shows no signs of losing her enthusiasm. She owns a house on Long Island and leads a very stable suburban life when she's not flying. Her neighbors must surely think it odd for a woman old enough to be a grandmother to leave home in a miniskirted uniform and fly to Saigon twice a month.

I once asked an attractive stewardess who had been flying for twenty years if she'd ever thought of quitting. "Not any longer than two minutes," she said. "What other job would pay me to go to Switzerland for two days a week? When I get there I rent a car and drive all around. I don't think there's a village in that whole beautiful country I haven't seen. As for the lakes and mountains . . ." Obviously, twenty years of travel haven't made a dent in this girl's curiosity or diminished her energy. Girls like this one and many others who have been flying longer than two years are truly professional, and my friend who is old enough to be a grandmother could run circles around most other women her age and a lot of us who are considerably younger.

But flying can become a kind of purgatory for girls who have lost their enthusiasm for travel and have no immediate prospects for marriage. They are plagued by an increasing boredom with the job and their lives—which, like boredom in any job, dulls the imagination and saps the energy. One intelligent stewardess who had been a kindergarten teacher confessed to me not long ago how unhappy she was. "I don't do anything but sit around and be bored. I guess I like to travel too much to give up flying, but I don't have much motivation to even take advantage of my passes on my free time. Everything just seems too much of an effort."

She had been flying for three years and was experiencing what most stewardesses call "the slump." The slump seems to be an unavoidable psychological malaise which creeps up on stewardesses after about two years of flying. It starts with depression, and if you don't catch yourself with some effective antidotes it can end in an overwhelming despair about life in general and what you're doing with it in particular. (You're serving all those irascible, indifferent, gullible *passengers.*) Its effects can be summed up by the sinking feeling that things can only get worse, and furthermore that they will all be blamed on you. Reactions to this depression can vary from the passive—such as one girl's melancholy wish for a tape recorder she could pin on her uniform which would repeat, "I'm sorry, I'm sorry, I'm sorry"—to the offensive—constant complaining about the job, or, even worse, sadistic treatment of passengers.

The director of one of the training schools I visited told me what a problem this condition is for the airlines. She also honestly admitted that she had gone through a severe attack of it herself when she had been flying. After months of committing all the sins of a bad stewardess she became disgusted with herself, shut herself in her room, and thought it all out. She came to the conclusion that most of her complaints against the world were really quarrels with herself. In her case, a little home therapy made life bearable again.

It does help to know that nearly all stewardesses who keep on flying go through the slump in varying degrees. And for many of them, realizing that they alone can solve the boredom of their lives serves to start them solving it.

You may be thinking that flying could never depress you, but that you aren't the stewardess *type*. If you meet the qualifications (the specific ones for each major United States airline are listed in Part II of this book), you really ought to consider whether or not you can be the type.

In general, the qualifications are:

1. Attractive appearance: by which is meant not beauty but neatness, proportionate weight to height, a good complexion, and a pleasant facial expression (good teeth framed by a smile).

2. Age: between 19½ and 26, although some airlines have no stated age limit, and will hire girls as old as 28.

3. Height: 5'2" to 5'9", but there are exceptions here also; Trans-East specializes in tiny stewardesses and won't hire you if you're over 5'1".

4. Vision requirements: these vary, some airlines hiring girls with 20/200 vision corrected by glasses or contact lenses; others restrict their requirements to eyesights no worse than 20/50 uncorrected.

5. Weight: proportionate to bone structure. Most airlines have recently liberalized their weight limits, some allowing up to 140 pounds for a tall girl.

6. Education: a high school diploma and two years of college or business experience is usual, but with the age minimum coming down to 19½, some airlines state only that college or working experience is desirable.

7. Marital status: requirements vary, but in general you must be single. TWA now hires married girls. Most airlines hire child-

less divorcees and widows, some hire those who are legally separated from their husbands.

8. Health: from my description of the job you must realize that you won't last long in it if you don't have a sturdy constitution. Every major airline gives you a physical before it hires you anyway.

9. Languages: domestic airlines don't require a second language; some international airlines do. If the airline flies both domestic and international routes, you may be hired for its domestic routes without speaking another language.

10. Nationality: many airlines hire non-United States citizens. Pan American, which must provide language-qualified girls for its round-the-world routes, has a high percentage of foreign nationals as stewardesses. They are constantly trying to find new ways of doing this within the increasingly strict limitations of the United States Immigration Department. The most recent method is to hire girls outside the United States on a D-3 visa, which requires the holder to leave the country every six weeks. Since the girls fly regularly out of the States, this presents no problem. Many domestic airlines are receptive to the applications of foreign girls who have a permanent visa.

I should say a word about the private schools which, heavily advertised, promise to prepare you for a career as an airline stewardess. Most major airlines prefer that applicants not waste their money on these schools. When an airline hires you it provides you with training at great expense. It would rather not have to undo any ideas and methods taught you by a private school. But there are exceptions. Western Airlines recruits many of its girls from the California State Junior Colleges, which offer stewardess-training preparation. Western also works closely with these colleges, and there are no conflicting ideas to undo when the girls are hired. Also, other, smaller, airlines, which don't have the budgets for extensive stewardess training, often do rely on private training schools to do some of the job for them.

I did fly with one girl who told me she would never have had the confidence to even apply to a major airline before she attended one of these schools. But keep in mind the fact that these schools, while very expensive, do not guarantee you a job as a stewardess. You would be well advised to apply to a few airlines before making the investment.

My own experiences in applying for this job certainly suggest that there really isn't a specific type of girl the airlines are looking for.

If it hadn't been for a friend of mine who had been a stewardess, I probably never would have considered this career. Mary Ellen, a rather impulsive girl, decided to tour Europe and try living in France when she got tired of flying. We met when we were both hired as service club directors on an Air Force base in northwest France. After a year of enjoying Europe she began to miss flying, and she finally left for home determined to go back to it.

I returned to New York soon after, thinking my urge to travel had been satisfied. I found an interesting job in a firm promoting international education and settled into my new life quite happily. My serenity lasted all of two months. I was appalled to find myself dreaming about Europe; after surveying my finances, I came to the gloomy conclusion that at the rate my savings were increasing I wouldn't see it again for years.

At the lowest point of my depression Mary Ellen flew into town, just out of stewardess training, spreading enthusiasm around like a contagious disease. She listened to my laments and told me to stop being ridiculous. I was a dope. "Why don't you fly to Europe and live in New York?"

"I'm not the type," I said, meaning, "They'd never hire me."

"If there's one thing I know," she said, "it's how to get hired by an airline. I've done it twice."

She then treated me to a crash course on how to get through an interview successfully; the main points to remember being: convince the interviewer you love people and travel, and smile, smile, smile.

Spurred on by visions of Paris and the lovely European countryside, I proceeded to Kennedy Airport. Not having investigated the relative merits of various airlines, I headed for the first one that I knew had European routes.

When I went into the hangar and requested an application

form, the receptionist immediately asked me in French how old I was. This unexpected turn of events threw me into a state of panic and I replied with the first French number that entered my mind, which luckily happened to be *vingt-et-un* (twenty-one) instead of fourteen or fifty. My random selection also happened to be a bare-faced lie. I was twenty-seven and never had any trouble recalling it in English.

Apparently I had passed some sort of bilingual examination, because she handed me an application. As I was preparing my smile, a man appeared and asked me into his office. I had put my correct age down on the application form; after looking over my answers, he shook his head. "Unfortunately, twenty-six is our maximum age limit, Miss Rich, but you seem to have all the other qualifications." Silence ensued as he studied first my age and then me. My smile became a grimace as the shores of France seemed more and more distant.

"Well," he said finally, "exceptions can sometimes be made. I'd like to discuss this with an associate." As he left the room France began to reappear, and my smile became sincere with relief. Ten minutes later, he returned. "Come and meet Miss Baldwin. If an exception is to be made, she'll have to agree."

Miss Baldwin looked at me coolly and asked me to sit down. At this moment, everything started going to pieces, beginning with my stockings. I'll never know whether they were actually a rotten pair of stockings or whether the ups and downs of my body temperature resulting from my emotional state destroyed their molecular structure. At any rate, I felt a zing go up my left leg. I shifted position so that the run was masked from Miss Baldwin's view, and got another zing for my trouble. Runner number two was in full view. My throat felt constricted, and I stopped talking in any comprehensible fashion. In rapid succession—zing, zing, zing—both stockings disintegrated before our very eyes. All I could think was that no airline stewardess would ever let her stockings treat her that way.

Fortunately, Miss Baldwin became warmer and kinder with every runner. Neither of us could bring ourselves to mention what was taking place on my legs. I was amazed to hear her say she agreed an exception could be made and tell me to go back to the other office. I walked airily back down the hall, not even trying to hide the offending stockings with my coat.

The man who'd sent me in to Miss Baldwin congratulated me and whipped out a medical form, which he began to fill in, saying, "I see you don't wear glasses and I assume you don't wear contact lenses." A rapid argument with myself ensued, gloomily decided in favor of honesty.

"Oh, but I do wear lenses," I said very softly, hoping he wouldn't hear me.

He sighed, looked at me, rolled his eyes, and shook his head. I stared back, still wearing my silly smile.

"You understand, I hope, that we were willing to make one exception in your case, Miss Rich, but I'm afraid we just can't make two. In view of the fact that you are not only past our age limit but have faulty eyesight as well, I'm afraid I'll have to say no."

Too old, too blind, I stumbled out into the parking lot, Europe disappearing behind a sea of tears. For a full five minutes I felt suicidal. That is, until my eyes began to focus on the opposite hangar of another international airline. Nothing to lose, I thought. I drove over and very cagily asked for information for a friend, me with my stockings hanging in shreds. I was handed some printed material which I pored over in the privacy of my car. I soon discovered a new reason for living—no maximum age limit. My admiration for this airline increased: what a sensible policy. My spirits really began to soar when I read, "contact lenses are allowed." Obviously, my employers and I were going to get along famously.

Two points seem worth making here. My experience with the first airline, however disappointing, does demonstrate that recruiting personnel are flexible to a point in interpreting the airline's requirements. And it is certainly true that not all airlines' qualifications are the same. My first interview was actually a masterpiece of mismanagement on my part, despite Mary Ellen's coaching. I should have investigated the requirements and routes of the different airlines and made some realistic decision as to preference in view of these facts. It is not unreasonable for an airline to expect you to know something about it before you apply; it can hardly be flattered if it concludes that you just closed your eyes and pointed to a spot on the yellow pages of your phone directory.

As for my perpetual smile, *that* was probably a good idea. From the applicant's point of view—certainly from mine—an always-present smile must feel strained and insincere after a while; but looking at it from the interviewer's point of view, a prospective stewardess's smile is one of her most important attributes. It is all a matter of economics to an airline. If they can depend on their cabin crews to smile and be pleasant despite personal moods which inspire scowls or even tears, passengers get a favorable impression—especially the kind of passenger who tends to interpret a frown as an indication of the engines' condition. Passengers usually return to airlines where they feel wanted and safe. Superficial or sincere, the smile is as necessary to a stewardess as legs are, and its effect should not be underestimated at any time.

It's a good idea to talk with a girl who flies for the airline you're applying to and find out what, besides the smile, is important to them. Often this isn't possible, which is why I have included such information in Part II of this book. In my case I phoned Mary Ellen, who produced a friend of hers working for the airline I was about to storm. I grilled the poor girl for hours, and by the time I finished with her I knew more about what this airline wanted than the interviewer.

I know from experience that it isn't just physical attributes but attitude and performance which determine the success of your interview. There isn't really a type, but there is an attitude, and it is quite simply possible to develop this attitude. A great many physically qualified girls are rejected because they give negative reasons for wanting to become a stewardess: "I don't like my job," or, "I'm bored with my life right now." The most desirable motives for wanting to fly are, first, that you enjoy working with people, and second, that you like or feel that you would like to travel. If you are in college, courses in psychology and sociology along with any extracurricular activities you can list strengthen your case. And working girls whose jobs have given them experience in dealing with the public are regarded favorably.

But the recruiter is interested mainly in whether or not you seem pleasant, calm, cooperative, attractive, and able to accept responsibility—in short, mature. If you convey these qualities without being aggressive or unduly nervous, your chances of being hired are excellent.

The best possible advice for a successful interview is to expect the unexpected. Be prepared to be disarmed by pleasant conversation and then—wham—find yourself suddenly asked a disconcerting question, intended to throw you into a state of confusion. I can't document this approach from my first interview, which was more than decent, but we had so many technical difficulties to occupy us that it can't be considered normal. But my experience during my second interview (along with many stories I've heard from other stewardesses) should give an idea of what I mean.

After my first interview, I felt nothing could faze me. (Although I did select my stockings very carefully before setting out.) The sheet I had been given informed me that interviewing began at 0900, at a hotel in Manhattan. Convinced that every other girl in New York would be out for my place in line, I arrived at quarter to nine, not caring if I seemed overanxious. Mrs. Reynolds, the interviewer, arrived at 0905, after I had worked myself into a nervous state wondering if I had the wrong day because I was the only one there. The interviewer actually seemed as glad to see me as I was to see her.

I liked her right away. In addition to being pleasant, she made me feel wanted. I know now that the fact that I was the only applicant to turn up in two weeks—a newspaper strike had prevented any public announcement of the interviews—had something to do with this agreeable state of affairs. We chatted for a while, and then she asked me to walk up and down the room and to show her my fingernails. First interviews often include this scene. If you need a five-foot area in which to swing your hips you'll never get up and down the aisle of an airplane, and chewed fingernails are forbidden.

I managed to keep the ubiquitous smile on my face without any effort, I was so relieved to find not even one beautiful creature waiting in line to shatter my confidence. The interviewer and I talked about such things as the newspaper strike until I was lulled into a state of complete relaxation.

Then came the bad moment. She suddenly asked me, "If you had three wishes, what would you wish for?" I nearly fell off my chair. Recovering, I masked my dismay in time to stammer an answer so saccharine that I have since repressed the details. It became obvious that this was one of those disconcerting questions she was obliged to ask. To her credit, I have to say that she actually blushed during the momentary stunned silence that followed it. Following my ridiculous reply, we resumed our impersonal and pleasant conversation with much relief on both sides.

But my experience was mild compared to that of a friend who told me that at the close of a very encouraging interview with a young man from TWA, he suddenly looked at her and said severely, "What would you say, Miss O'Hanlon, if I told you that you will never be a stewardess for TWA?" She went white, then answered weakly that she would probably apply to another airline. The interviewer let her eyes fill with tears before he smiled and said, "The reason I say that is that TWA doesn't have stewardesses; we call our girls 'hostesses.' How would you like to be a hostess for TWA?" She restrained herself from saying, "How would you like a punch in the nose?" and smiled back sweetly in the affirmative.

Some interviewers use the aggressive "prove yourself" technique, which can be upsetting if you aren't prepared to justify yourself. One stewardess told me her interview was a real test in self-control. The interviewer was so disagreeable that she gave up all hope before they were half finished. Fortunately she didn't take his mood personally, but kept responding calmly. When he asked, "What makes you think *you* would be a good airline stewardess?" she simply said, "It's hard to say anything for sure about what I'm like, so I depend on the reactions of my friends. They tell me that I'm understanding, helpful, easy to get along with. I hope that's true. I think I would like this job and would try to be good at it." The interviewer jumped up, rapped his desk, and said, "Good, you're hired." She was completely taken aback by this sudden switch in mood, and to this day wonders if he was nursing a hangover, fed up with his job, on the verge of a nervous breakdown, or just putting her on.

Airlines may consider the interviewing trick of following pleasant conversation with a very personal and/or inane question a necessary test of reactions: it happens to be a situation with which stewardesses are faced all the time. For one thing, people who find themselves in unfamiliar and perhaps frightening surroundings often act in an uncharacteristic manner. (My mother, normally a soft-spoken woman, is convinced when traveling that if she shouts loud enough foreigners will understand her English without any previous knowledge of the language.) On an airplane, anxiety may often overcome common sense. I'm not talking about difficult passengers, just the ones who politely inquire if they can open the window at 36,000 feet. In any case, the ability to improvise appropriate and soothing responses to a startling question or situation is certainly important to a stewardess.

How much *pleasure* is taken in throwing an applicant into a state of confusion depends, of course, on the interviewer. Mrs. Reynolds obviously didn't enjoy it at all. But reports I've had from other stewardesses are much more in accordance with what I had imagined and prepared myself for—interviews overcrowded and nerve-shattering if you don't happen to feel you are the most marvelous girl in the room, and who ever does? Few girls are so self-confident that they can enter a room overfilled with beautiful creatures and not feel slightly eclipsed.

The fact is, beauty is probably the least important factor in being hired as an airline stewardess. This is easily proved by taking a look around an airline terminal, where you are likely to see many stewardesses, few of whom will be close to beautiful. The reason for the difference in beauty ratio between applicants and stewardesses is simple: too many of the beauties who applied didn't qualify in more important areas. So the airlines end up with a cross section of looks, including some plain, many attractive, and a few beautiful girls.

It is clear from my experience and that of other stewardesses that it is sometimes necessary to try two or more airlines before finding the one that wants you. There really isn't one strict set of rules for recruiters to follow, and often they can seem as arbitrary, within the framework of general qualifications, as the weather. I overheard one conversation in which a recruiter admitted he'd turned down a qualified applicant because she reminded him of an old girl friend who had dropped him. Remember, interviewers are subject to moods and inexplicable actions just as often as the rest of us. It is even possible to be rejected on the first try with an airline and accepted by it when a different interviewer comes around.

There are many variables which determine final selections, one of the most important being the number of trainees needed. New stewardesses are always more in demand in the summertime than at any other time of the year. Consequently, late winter and early spring are usually the best times to apply.

Very often airlines make a concerted effort to hire many girls at once. You may then be informed that there will be a one- to four-month wait before you will be sent to training. So the earlier you apply in the winter, the higher you are on the list to be assigned your training date. Girls about to graduate should apply several months before, so they will be trained before the summer is over. If you start flying in the summer, your chances of holding a bid are much better than in the winter, when you will certainly be on reserve more often.

As final advice I offer here a check list for review before you go to an airlines interview:

1. Dress simply—no avant-garde fashions at this time, no matter how stylish or becoming.

2. Use conservative make-up—the natural look, which every fashion magazine has instructions on how to achieve.

3. Wear your hair simply, and make sure its color at least *looks* natural.

4. Practice a graceful walk and be conscious of your posture.

5. Practice speaking in a low, well-modulated voice.

6. Look the interviewer in the eye, respond calmly to questions, don't interrupt, and don't be negative in your reasons for wanting to fly. I have already recommended "enjoy travel and working with people" as the most uncomplicated and, I hope, honest answer to that question.

7. Have some activities, work experience, or courses you can mention which will help convince the interviewer that you mean the above.

8. Have a practice interview with a friend. Let her ask you all the difficult questions and see how you respond. Then you won't be startled by the sound of your own voice during the real interview.

9. Don't be nervous; assume they need you.

10. SMILE, SMILE, SMILE.

5

FIVE WEEKS CAN BE A LONG TIME:
Training Without Tears

Now that the interview is over, unless you were hired on the spot —which is very unusual—there will be a nervous waiting period before you hear the verdict. I was told after a week's interval that I had been hired and would be informed at a later date as to when I'd begin training. A long month later, I received a letter instructing me to appear at the training school at the end of May. This meant three more months would pass before I could leave the ground, but I was so happy at the prospect of travel in my future that nothing could have dampened my enthusiasm.

Certainly, nothing could have prepared me for the transformation I was to undergo before getting anywhere near an airplane. I have never been very enthusiastic about overwhelmingly feminine atmospheres like sororities and beauty salons—in fact, I react like a claustrophobic trapped in an elevator. I realize that most girls enjoy this sort of environment and find it relaxing. I mention my prejudices only because they can't help but color my interpretation of the following events—airline training schools combine all the qualities, good and bad, of a sorority house and a beauty parlor.

My account of training should be prefaced with some generalizations about the evolution of airline training schools in the past ten years. The major United States airlines have invested a great deal of money creating what some refer to as training colleges. For the most part they have attempted to outdo each other in making their schools glamorous, luxurious, and convenient. I have recently traveled around the country visiting twelve of them, and can say only that things have changed very much for the better since I attended mine a few years ago.

All of them provide comfortable living quarters and well-equipped classrooms. At the very least you are given a pleasant room (air-conditioned when necessary—not the case in my day), which you share with one to four girls. Almost all of the schools provide you with private baths, laundry rooms, TV, hair dryers, and maid service. Depending on the airline, the facilities vary from perfectly adequate all the way to glamorous complexes which could compete with expensive beauty spas—heated swimming pools, beautifully landscaped grounds, game rooms, tennis courts, dazzlingly equipped exercise rooms, and even saunas. Since you are there only from three and a half to six weeks, it would be rather silly to choose an airline just because it has one of these expensive training schools, but if it turns out that yours does, you'll have found an early fringe benefit of this career.

Uniform designs have also changed since I began flying. The airlines have been competing with each other in fashionable uniform design, with varying degrees of success. And since fashion now dictates—may this be the last time I use this phrase—that every woman do her own thing, airlines are even giving girls a choice in uniform colors, accessories, and hair style. Individuality is blossoming to such a degree, in fact, that if I see one more stewardess with a towering Marie Antoinette hairdo, its sausage curls wilting into limp strands, I may turn reactionary and agitate for a return to the pageboy.

All these decisions about how to express one's individuality weren't a problem during *my* training. In 1963, the airlines still hadn't emerged from the 1950's as far as fashion *and* training were concerned. For five weeks, I discovered, I was going to have to keep my mind in a straitjacket and my emotions completely repressed.

There is still an enormous amount of material to be assimilated in a very short time, of course. Formerly the airlines accomplished this task by constant repetition. The result was almost stupefying. Methods have changed quite a bit now: there are more observation flights, visual and educational-aid devices, and huge complexes where the girls are given more complete mock-ups of airplanes, so

71

that they learn by performing rather than by rote. Some airlines send trainees out on flights during their first week to observe and even help out. This does seem to be the most efficient way of learning a stewardess's duties. The reality of performance fixes the methods of service in your mind infinitely quicker than memorizing baffling lists which make no real sense until you see things in operation.

The mechanics of a stewardess's job are not difficult. It is largely a matter of organization, and knowing where everything can be found. Learning the service is, in fact, hardly more challenging than elementary school would be for a high school graduate. Easy but tedious.

However, there is great presure put on you to concentrate on hundreds of details at once, and it is not uncommon for girls to torture themselves during training, convinced that it is going to be impossible for them to grasp all of it. Some instructors' attitudes don't help—they may continually remind you of how much you have to learn, pointing out that if you fail to be serious about it, dismissal is certain. I've seen girls who were certainly capable of mastering where to find the spoons and how long to cook a steak become so panicky about being dismissed that they could hardly remember their own names.

Most instructors realize this problem, but if yours doesn't, let me say this for all of them: please relax. It is a major problem to get out of the bed in the morning if you convince yourself that you are about to meet your doom that day. You wouldn't have been hired if the airline didn't need you and want you to survive training.

As for me, I managed to avoid hysteria but did find one part of training a seemingly endless torment: the beauty instruction. I have to say that most girls thoroughly enjoyed it, and would probably find it even more delightful today now that more individuality is allowed. But my neuroses about beauty salons—which I can just barely gather enough courage to visit approximately three times a year—made the experience excruciating for me.

The first day of class, our looks were appraised by a group of instructors whose taste in make-up was light years away from mine. Now, I not only have strong negative feelings about beauty salons, but tubes of baby blush and bottles of snowy peach foundation make my skin itch. And my eyes begin to water and blink uncontrollably when I look at false eyelashes.

I listened dutifully to the beauty instructor's advice about the female complexion's need for efficient moisturizers to protect it from the weather and the very drying atmosphere inside an airplane. I am sure this is sound advice for most women—high altitudes and pressurization dehydrate one's system, and many airline stewardesses develop dry skin after they begin flying. But for me it wasn't: after two years of creaming and moisturizing, I developed the most appalling skin condition—I who had never had a blemish, even during my teens. My doctor laughingly informed me that I had developed a case of adult acne—flying had for some strange reason given me oily skin. It seems that even physically I am contrary by nature.

But at the first beauty session I still had fairly dry skin. I viewed the boxes, bottles, and tubes with alarm. We were instructed to make ourselves up in a certain way, with a great deal of help from our individual teachers. When they were finished with us we looked like a regiment of Barbie dolls. To make matters worse, the eye shadow provided was a rather sickly green, which tended to make those of us with faintly sallow skin look as if we had contracted hepatitis. During the make-up period my usually rosy cheeks had turned ashen white—the instructor told me peevishly that I "drained color," and kept applying rouge until I looked like Pierrette.

I was able to keep smiling, until they sent us to a beauty salon to have our hair styled. I went, of course, in a spirit of resignation mixed with acute depression: I had the distinct feeling that they would insist on giving me a permanent. (I had just spent a whole glorious year on vacation from the hairdresser growing all my hair out to the same length, and wore it straight.) But the stylist, after giving me a quick look, startled me beyond belief by announcing, "I like your hair the way it is." I blinked at him. "So do I," I said, and fled—before I found out it was all a trick.

The weather in the Midwest in May and June is positively steamy. I desperately tried to disguise myself as a Barbie doll—

rolling my hair in curlers every night and making it slightly bouffant by back-combing it, a process which affects me like fingernails screeching across a blackboard—but all efforts proved fruitless. By the end of the day my hair hung limp and straight.

After a few moist days, my beauty instructor clucked her tongue and said my hair simply wouldn't do, it was too long. Fortunately (she said), a stylist was coming the next day to give a class in setting and combing. I prayed for my sane stylist friend, but this one turned out to be a birdlike little man who summoned me into the middle of the mirror-walled room and as he surveyed me, said menacingly, "My, my, you do need a cut."

That was the last time he looked at my hair until he had finished. He proceeded to seize a pair of scissors in one hand and pieces of my hair in the other and chop haphazardly all over my head. Paralyzed with horror, I watched him flirting with himself in the mirror while I began to look more and more like St. Joan. When he finished I had a crew cut. I think even he was shocked with the results. He looked at me accusingly, as if I had done the cutting myself, and said, "Well, that's about the best we can do with that."

After class, the beauty instructor said firmly, "It's too straight." Having been rendered mute by the haircut, I silently went off to have the dreaded permanent. When I emerged from the hairdryer hours later, the top of my head recalled not St. Joan so much as deep-fried parsley. In the next day's summer heat, my hair proceeded to go limp and curly instead of limp and straight. At the grooming class I got a dubious look: "You don't know how to set and comb your hair correctly. Tomorrow morning come to class with your hair in curlers." That instruction almost did me in. I would have to travel from the apartments where we were living to the training center, by bus, with my hair in *curlers*. She might just as well have asked me to wear an ankle bracelet too. I began to feel my identity slipping away.

It must be emphasized that I did not argue with her, nor did I betray any of the surliness and rage simmering inside me. I simply went back to my room and screamed incoherently at my image in the mirror while I tried to make the rollers stay in my hair. I finally ended up drinking the beer with which I was setting my hair, although it was forbidden to drink in the room.

Not more than a few hundred people stopped, stared, or pointed at me when I took the bus to class the next morning with my hair sporting bright-pink rollers. The beauty instructor came in the mirrored room armed with a can of hair spray—it was fingernail-on-the-blackboard-time again. Hair spray makes me choke and my eyes water. She grabbed a hair brush and I took off my kerchief. All the rollers fell out at the same time—I had virtually no hair to pin them to. She regarded them disapprovingly for a moment and then started trying to back-comb my hair. She fast came to the conclusion that there was hardly any hair to back-comb and said, "Well, it's just too short to do anything with." I suppressed an urge to run screaming from the room.

Eventually she stopped complaining, just in the nick of time, because I was near the breaking point. Her arrangement of my hair can best be described as a fright wig bought in a witch's cut-rate store—all pieces sticking out in various directions sprayed into plastic stiffness with the aerosol bomb of glue which seemed to be a permanent extension of her hand. When I looked at myself in the mirror, I was really frightened—my eyes were glittering madly, my smile was definitely a sinister sneer, and my face was framed by clumps of hair in a Medusa-like design. The effect couldn't help but make the beauty instructor slightly uneasy. I think she finally got the message that things had gone too far. (That might explain why she avoided any direct communication with me for the rest of training.) My hair went back to hanging limp and curly, and was studiously ignored. The only indication that they still gave any thought to my beauty problems was a certain melancholy look—the kind a mother might give a retarded child—when their gaze wandered from my ever-present smile to my funny-looking hairdo.

This bitter experience was my greatest test of endurance. The physical damage wasn't permanent; fortunately, hair grows back and make-up washes off. It was the psychological effect which nearly broke me. The instructors apparently saw me as an inept misfit who just wouldn't respond to their good-hearted attempts to make her into one of the cookie-pattern replicas they regularly turn out with brisk efficiency. Actually, they were right, I guess, but they had no idea of the dreams of rebellion which, fortunately for my future, remained locked inside of me. The fact that I didn't resist any of their attempts to transform me and even tried to appear helpful was the only thing that saved me from being drummed out of the ranks.

Although I still hear tales of woe from new stewardesses, I haven't heard one recently that could match mine. The most serious have been complaints from girls whose skin reacted badly to the foundation they were required to use. One told me she had put one small dab on each cheek so she could say honestly, "Yes, I'm using it," until training was over and she could throw it away. A few airlines require the use of a particular brand of cosmetics during training, but most let you choose the one that agrees with your skin. This *can* work out in your favor if you like the brand they require, because often you may continue buying it through the airline at a considerable discount.

Although it's true that hair-length regulations are more lenient now, don't let your hopes soar about keeping your waist-length hair. Count on its being cut to perhaps an inch or two below your collar, and then later, if you are clever enough to conceal longer hair in a chignon or knot, you can be happy. Many training schools offer hairpieces at a discount price, and the instructors will show you how to manage them.

I don't want to dampen your spirits any more, but you might be well advised to stop worrying about your hair during training and begin to consider your legs when flying. One of the common hazards of this career is varicose veins. You are likely to be walking around just after a plane has taken off and is still climbing. The ascent forces blood down to your legs, and after a while, if you have a tendency to weak blood vessels, varicose veins will raise their ugly heads. Depending on how severe the weakness is, this condition can vary from a few unsightly veins to painful leg aches or worse. The best safeguards are to try and stay in your seat as long as the plane is climbing (seldom possible because most captains turn off the seat belt sign right away and too much work must be done in too short a time), and to wear support hose.

Support hose comes in attractive colors and textures now and is well worth its cost, which is reasonable if you stock up at a discount store in your base city or a city you fly to. A senior stewardess can tell you where, if you don't know. And if your airline requires that you wear a girdle (which most don't now), support panty hose gives you a light girdle without the discomfort.

One girl taught me a trick which to my mind rivals the invention of sliced bread. "You don't have to throw away your support panty hose just because you run one leg," she said. "Cut off the leg with the run and save the rest so you can make two bad pairs into one good pair. The two panty parts you wear on top of each other and will *really* work like a girdle." I thanked her for the tip, kicked myself for the money I'd wasted, and started following her advice for *all* my panty hose.

Please don't think that all this advice on how to survive the make-up, hair, and girdle traumas without actually breaking the regulation is meant to encourage insubordination. This is a tendency which must be suppressed throughout training. But there are ways of solving minor problems without resorting to slavish obedience or drawing undue attention to yourself—which should be avoided at all costs. And, there is certainly some useful beauty advice given trainees. Today's more natural styles for hair and make-up might even make the beauty instruction enjoyable for a maverick like me. And the training schools that provide saunas and all kinds of fascinating apparatus for exercise seem like a little bit of heaven to me. Ah, what a sauna could have done to calm my nerves then!

There is one problem I never had in training, simply because I was blessed with light bone structure—weight. A stewardess would never be hired in the first place if her figure weren't in proportion to her height, but the regulations become more stringent once training begins. Each airline has a weight chart by height, and the scale has the authority of the voice of God. You may not look or feel overweight, but if the scale says you are, you are given a diet and the warning that if those pounds don't come off you won't see graduation.

To give you some idea of what a weight chart has in store for you, here is one from Northeast Airlines:

HEIGHT	WEIGHT	MAXIMUM HIP SIZE
5'2"	101–115 lbs.	34"
5'3"	105–118 lbs.	34"
5'4"	108–120 lbs.	35"
5'5"	111–125 lbs.	36"
5'6"	115–130 lbs.	36"
5'7"	118–133 lbs.	37"
5'8"	121–136 lbs.	38"
5'9"	125–138 lbs.	38"

You will see in Part II that most airlines allow a maximum of 140 pounds, but in general this chart is a good one to test yourself by. If you have always had a weight problem, try to look on the bright side. Since it is necessary to maintain the proper weight throughout your flying career, the discipline could reform some bad eating habits for good and—if you can project that far into the future— keep you slender while all your friends are getting a middle-age spread. Some newspaper articles have claimed that ex-airline stewardesses as a group are younger-looking and in better physical shape than other women in their age group, if that's any consolation for not eating your dessert. One article even gives this as one reason for the low divorce rate among stewardesses.

Weight checks, of course, are only one of many restrictions and regulations the airline trainee must put up with. And the sometimes strict surveillance and dormitory hours can seem extremely confining to girls who have enjoyed the freedom of their own apartments. (It's only temporary, but if feeling confined drives you bats, you'd better think twice before you apply for the job.) Under the frequently glamorous trappings of some training schools, one can detect a faintly penitentiary atmosphere—particularly when you're informed about the electrically alarmed fences, the night watchmen, the windows which automatically lock at 10 P.M. The airlines have developed a perhaps not unfounded suspicion that precautions are necessary to keep intruders out, not the girls in. Also, they feel that the curfew regulations are not unreasonable. They do ensure that trainees spend most of their time studying and not playing when a few thousand dollars are being invested to teach each girl how to represent the airline to its customers.

Not all airline-training schools have strict dormitory regulations. Some of them feel the girls should be mature enough to police themselves. It doesn't really matter. You are in class from nine or even eight till five in the evening, and at night during the week you have so much material to go over that you are unlikely to have the time or energy for late dates. You may feel that the restrictions of your training school are silly, but it would be even sillier to be dismissed for breaking them. It is, after all, only a month or so.

In general, airlines believe that team effort is the most important lesson they are teaching prospective stewardesses. If a girl can't work with other people smoothly and efficiently, the job is just that much harder for her fellow stewardesses, but more importantly, the stewardess on an airplane is responsible not only for service but for the safety of the passengers in an emergency. In this sense it is a matter of life or death for the airlines to stress the importance of teamwork and conformity to regulations.

This attitude unfortunately can amount to an obsession with some training personnel, who seem ready to interpret disregard of a minor regulation as a threat to the life of a passenger. Although most instructors are reasonable people with a sane and flexible approach to their jobs, I wouldn't test their flexibility during training. You just might pick the wrong one. And being flip about any aspect of your training is likely to make your seriousness about your responsibilities suspect—don't do it, no matter how ridiculous things may appear to you. The idiotic mistakes you'll inevitably make at first will be forgiven if you will patiently tolerate sometimes tedious seriousness about every petty detail you're taught, from manicures to how to carry your handbag.

You may consider many instructions an insult to your intelligence—or unforgivably square. But remember: the course was developed to train thousands of girls of varying intelligence; and airlines, which exist to transport passengers *safely* from one place to another, are of necessity conservative.

Your constant companion during training will be a big notebook, "the manual." You will carry this manual with you all day, not only because you are required to but because it becomes a kind of security blanket—all the regulations and procedures are contained in it, and if you think you have confused something, a quick look at the facts can be very reassuring.

And all the little speeches you will have to make on the airplane are right there for you to practice word for word on the public address system. If you are nervous about microphones, you'll eventually get over it when you realize almost everyone else is, too. Hearing bad speech patterns magnified over the PA can give you added incentive to stop mumbling, talking through your nose, or letting your voice zoom up to unpleasantly high registers. When you have been flying for a short while, all the agony over the PA will be forgotten, and you will know these spiels as well as your own name. Just don't let yourself get bored with them and improvise to the extent one girl did while making an announcement about the sound of the landing gear being lowered and locked into position for a landing in Chicago: "Ladies and gentlemen, the sound you just heard was the sound of your baggage being lowered and dropped into Lake Michigan."

During training you are also taught such very useful information as *why* an airplane flies. I have at times memorized these simple scientific explanations, promptly forgetting them a day later. I resist remembering, not because I am antiscience but because flying has always seemed a magical phenomenon to me. I suppose I prefer viewing it with my unknowledgeable enchantment to reducing it to a formula.

You will doubtless be surprised to discover how little you remember of the geography of the United States, unless you've brushed up ahead of time. As I remember, every cheek in the class turned pink when we were passed a blank map of the United States and asked to identify each state. Some airlines send out helpful material to trainees before they arrive, with self-teaching aids for learning airport code names, the twenty-four-hour clock, and forgotten geography. This saves time and, in the case of the geography, in-class embarrassment.

Every training school has a different curriculum, but you can depend on not having more than an hour for lunch and not more than ten-minute intervals between classes if that. Some airlines give an hour a day of beauty instruction, and others, like Northwest, who likes its stewardesses farm-fresh, give only two hours in the whole five weeks.

Although instructors continually stress the seriousness of all the information trainees must assimilate, they do give the girls every chance to pass their tests. They patiently answer the same questions over and over again, and if a girl has trouble concentrating because of nervousness, they will work with her until she calms down and masters the material. Whether nervous or confident, you should always ask for an explanation if you have questions about material you don't understand. Instructors who have to teach the same dry material to each class are likely to be more bored with it than you are, so they welcome questions.

Most airlines advise that girls bring from two to three hundred dollars with them to training, to cover expenses before they begin receiving their pay and expense checks. (The first regular paycheck comes after you've been flying two or three weeks.) Airlines which house their trainees in motels arrange a special low price for them, but hotel bills and meals usually have to be paid before any money comes in from the airline. It's important that you plan for these expenses—financial worries are the last thing you need during training.

Prepare yourself, also, for the possibility of not being based in a city you had your heart set on. You can give yourself some realistic idea of the junior bases by asking the interviewer, and hope she answers you accurately. But sometimes the situation changes from month to month so that you may unintentionally be misled. I kept paying rent on my apartment in New York during training because the instructors told me there was a good chance that I would be based there. By some unlucky twist of fate there were only two bases available when I graduated; the week before and the week after, New York was open—but not for my graduating class.

The available bases are usually awarded by seniority based on age, sometimes by class grade or by lot. And often, as is the case with the smaller airlines, only one base is ever available. This fact being known ahead of time, you're at least spared unrealistic dreaming and consequent disappointment.

If you *are* disappointed with your assigned base, you can transfer as soon as there are openings, after you have been employed for six months. Of course, it depends on what's available, but it is rare that a girl can't find one base she likes, even if it isn't her first choice. You wouldn't be attracted to this job if you weren't adjustable.

Having made it through training until graduation day, you'll be so happy to pack up and start flying that it really doesn't matter what kind of ceremony sends you off. Some graduations are elaborate and sentimental, with champagne luncheons for you and any family who can attend. Others are short and completed by sweet rolls and coffee. In the ever-present spirit of competition, more and more airlines are providing the elaborate kind—a nice touch, though hardly necessary.

All in all, training can be enjoyable if you look on it as a rest from the demands of the outside world and just concentrate on the demands of learning the material at hand. The comfortable to luxurious living conditions temporarily insulate and isolate you from the kind of life you have been leading. It's true that you may share your pleasant room with three to four other girls—the only thing to do is to consider yourself part of a group for five weeks and make the necessary adjustment to the lack of privacy.

While doing research for this book, I showed up at one training college during graduation. At a champagne luncheon the airline threw for the trainees and their guests, I sat next to a girl who told me in a soft Southern drawl how *much* she'd enjoyed training. "It was interesting and fun," she said, then sighed and added, "but I sure am glad it's over. I reckon I couldn't stand it one more day."

Five weeks can be a long time.

6

IN CASE OF EMERGENCY, PLEASE
DO NOT REMOVE CABIN ATTENDANTS
FROM THE AIRCRAFT

Most passengers don't realize or even want to think about the fact that those miniskirted girls who serve them their drinks and meals are responsible for their lives if anything goes wrong. You may not have thought about it, either, but the most important training stewardesses receive is in what to do in the event of an emergency.

I have great admiration for the methods airlines use to instruct trainees in the fundamentals of emergency procedures. The courses are taught by especially well qualified people who manage to go over the grisly details of airplane crashes without scaring you half to death *or* underplaying the possible consequences.

You must learn the very strict regulations and procedures set up by the Federal Aviation Agency, must successfully perform precise in-flight drills, and must pass a yearly test, or be dismissed. There is no leniency here, because it is a matter of life and death.

Every stewardess must know where all the emergency equipment can be found on all the types of aircraft her airline operates. This includes exits, slides, fire extinguishers, oxygen bottles and masks, first-aid kits, megaphones, and for overwater flights the life vest, rafts, and all the paraphernalia inside them. This is, of course, simply a matter of memorizing. However, you must also know how to operate all this equipment, some of it unwieldy and very heavy (life rafts, for instance). Emergency courses include drills with the equipment until each girl can handle and operate every item to the satisfaction of her company and the FAA. Still, the drills aren't really difficult—just a matter of practice, and there is ample opportunity for that during training.

Most airlines don't skimp on facilities, to ensure that each girl becomes familiar with all aspects of airline safety. Trainees inflate and jump down slides, open window exits, and climb out on airplane wings. Those who are going to fly over water have to prove they have the courage to jump into deep water and *then* inflate their life vests, have to drag life rafts through airplanes, and operate the rafts in swimming pools or even in lakes, better simulating the conditions of a plane ditching in the ocean. And there is an amazing amount of hardware and survival equipment stored in each life raft—a radio transmitter, canopy, flashlight, mirror, flares, dyes, water purifiers, navigation equipment, and Charm candies, to name just a few. Each girl must demonstrate that she can operate the equipment—and remember the order of importance of her duties during an emergency ditching.

Knowing how to handle any emergency, from a sick passenger to a crash landing, is impressed on every stewardess not only during training but throughout her career. With the boom in air travel, and a much greater fund of knowledge about airline safety, the airlines and the FAA now work together in setting up regulations and procedures which get stricter every year. Up until 1967, the FAA required every airline to physically demonstrate that a load of passengers could be evacuated from each type of aircraft operated—using only half of the available exits—in not more than two minutes. At that time the airlines suggested to the FAA that the time be cut to ninety seconds.

Perhaps the most sobering experience in your training comes when you have a drill to evacuate fellow trainees who pose as real passengers—the blind, paraplegic, or pregnant, children and elderly people—under conditions which might occur in a real crash: inoperative exits, slides put in upside down, panicky passengers. All in ninety seconds.

Even under these simulated conditions there is a disturbing amount of panic and confusion which brings home the deadly importance of emergency training. And even the most blasé stewardesses find these drills attention-riveting.

As well as learning and practicing your duties in an emergency, you are lectured and shown films of plane crashes, ditchings, in-flight fires, first aid, and a grimly funny one on the effects of lack of oxygen—which produces, before brain damage or death, a ridiculous state of apparent drunkenness. The passengers in the movie put food in their eyes, noses, and ears; women apply lipstick all over their faces, and when shown their actions on film afterward have no recollection of abnormal behavior.

Along with all the alarming realities about emergencies, stewardesses learn some reassuring information about the safety of flying and the skill of the cockpit crews. There is continual war among statisticians as to how much safer—if at all—air travel is than other means of transportation. I couldn't begin to unravel the complications and contortions of the statistical analyses, but I do know that I am far more afraid of driving than flying. You might consider this crazy bit of information: it would take a passenger more than eighty years of flying twenty-four hours a day before he could statistically expect a fatal injury in an airplane crash. And airline pilots pay a lower life insurance premium than bartenders or doctors. If the insurance companies, famously conservative in their estimates of possible life spans, think I'm safer in an airplane than in a bar or hospital, I'll take their word for it.

Most airplane crashes occur during landing or take-off. As a consequence, most fatalities are the result of smoke inhalation and fire rather than injuries on impact. The Air Line Pilots Association, a crusader for greater air safety, did a study of 682 crashes involving the five largest United States airlines between 1938 and 1961. The committee reported that 73 percent (almost 500) of the accidents resulted in no fatalities despite the fact that the aircraft were totally destroyed or critically damaged by fire.

The important point for the prospective stewardess is that by far the large majority of airplane crashes are survivable—a fact which the majority of passengers refuse to believe. And crucial to the passenger survival rate is the way the stewardesses, pilots, *and* passengers react under emergency conditions.

Obviously, then, the main problem a stewardess must contend with in emergencies is her own response and that of the passengers. Airlines are determined to avoid tragedies like the one which happened in Denver in 1960 when a stewardess opened her exit after a crash landing, inflated the slide, and jumped down it, shouting behind her, "Follow me." Unfortunately some forty-odd passengers suffering from panic and confusion didn't hear her and stayed in their seats—where they were overcome by smoke inhalation, *not* fire. If the stewardess had remembered her training and kept her head, the majority of those passengers would have survived.

I should point out that there is a much more impressive record of stewardesses who have shown courage and reliability in performing their duties, some even losing their lives to save passengers. But the airlines don't want *any* blots on their records in this area.

A trainee learns many interesting facts about the way people react during emergencies. Like everything else, even these reactions seem to change with the temper of the times and the increasing sophistication of air travelers. In 1964, only 10 percent of the nation's population had taken a flight on a scheduled airliner. By 1970, 60 percent will have flown, though only about 15 percent of these take more than one or two flights a year. The 15 percent is made up of businessmen, who take 50 percent of all flights. This means that although more people are flying every year, at least half of the passenger loads comprise experienced flyers who make more than five trips annually.

When I was in training in 1963, there was great concern about the passivity of passengers during emergencies. There were too many alarming instances of passengers just sitting in their seats after a crash and dying from smoke inhalation, as in the Denver crash. Stewardesses were instructed then to remember to do anything that would get people on their feet and away from the airplane—including shouting, pushing, pulling, and kicking. Anything to make the passengers move.

At my last yearly emergency review, we were all informed that there has been a trend to quick action on the part of passengers, sometimes too quick. There was one instance when a stewardess who had just flung the door open after a crash landing was picked up by a very hefty passenger and tucked under his arm like a football. He raced off the airplane with her for a touchdown, shouting, "You shouldn't be here!" Fortunately the other passengers were following fast on his heels, because she was certainly supposed to be there to help them off.

This case prompted a suggestion for a sign to be installed by each emergency exit: IN CASE OF EMERGENCY, PLEASE DO NOT REMOVE CABIN ATTENDANTS FROM THE AIRCRAFT.

Even more alarming than being spirited off an airplane before finishing the job is the case of a stewardess who was kneeling in the exit to inflate the slide. Before she could stand up three men had used her as a door mat. Then there was another stewardess in the same position who, before she even got a chance to inflate the slide, found herself kicked quite a few feet out and down, face first, in the mud—for which she was grateful because it could have been concrete.

Yes, some passengers have become very active during emergencies, and one can only conclude that this is a mixed blessing. Active panic can be as dangerous as passive panic, as is illustrated by the case of a stewardess who was unable to open an emergency exit because passengers were crushing her up against the door— making it impossible for her to pull the door *in* first, in order to open it out.

Of course, the passengers couldn't be expected to know that aircraft doors must rotate inward about six inches before they can be pushed out and open. This design eliminates any chance of the door being sucked open during flight—the greater air pressure inside the plane forces the door against the fusilage, providing a more foolproof seal than any of the mechanical locks already on them.

There is some information passengers *can* be expected to know, but discouragingly few of them do. Airlines, well aware that passengers react much more neurotically to the possible dangers of traveling by air than, for instance, by car, use a soft-sell approach in providing emergency information on the airplane. The result is that very few passengers listen to the stewardess when she gives the oxygen mask demonstration, points out the emergency exits, and directs their attention to the emergency information in the seat pockets in front of them. This information is supposed to be given with authority and in a soothing voice—a rather impossible combination.

A perfect example of the passengers' lack of attention to this information is the case of an exasperated stewardess who informed her passengers: "In the unlikely event of depressurization, the oxygen mask will fall in front of you. Take the mask in your hand, attach it to your navel, and breathe normally." Not one passenger laughed at this ridiculous instruction, because none of them was listening in the first place.

There is the problem not only of apathy but often of open hostility from passengers in understanding their role in air safety. This makes the airlines reluctant to try to impress it on them in more than a cursory manner. How many times have we heard, "Well, Blank Airline lets us bring three suitcases to every seat"? The FAA and the airlines initiated some important new regulations in 1967 which, when enforced, make air travel safer. Unfortunately, passenger reaction to the regulations which affect them range from annoyance to hysteria.

You will probably recognize some of these recent regulations:

1. No carry-on luggage to be permitted on the airplane which won't fit under the seats. This regulation is the one which caused most of the screams and hostility. It's an important one: during a crash, unsecured objects can become lethal missiles flying through the cabin; they are also a major cause of injury during severe turbulence. The passenger who refused to observe these regulations would probably be the first to sue the company if he suffered a concussion or a broken limb when hit by his own baggage.

2. All seat backs must be in an upright position during landing and take-off. How uncomfortable and silly—unless you happen to be in a crash, where an upright seat could prevent a serious back injury and also facilitate the evacuation of the passenger behind you.

3. The emergency procedure information in every seat pocket must explain the different types of emergency equipment and positions of emergency exits on that particular aircraft. Previously this information included diagrams of equipment on all the types of aircraft flown by the airline—much too confusing for a passenger, who might not know what kind of airplane he was on. But if I had a dollar for every passenger who reads this information, I doubt if my taxes would increase much.

To add to the passengers' irritation, airlines are installing restraining rails under each seat, which cuts down on storage space and causes confusion as to how to get the baggage under the seat in the first place. More cause for aggravation, but those metal bars prevent baggage from hurtling forward during an accident to crush legs of passengers. In the past, it was not uncommon to see suitcases and briefcases zooming down the entire length of the aircraft on a landing if the reverse thrust of the engines brought the airplane to abrupt deceleration.

These new regulations, then, should have been welcomed by passengers; needless to say, they were not. The regulations are only as good as the enforcement of them, and the miniskirted stewardess must be the policeman. To add a nursery-school atmosphere to the already regressive behavior of some of the passengers, stewardesses often find themselves going through an enormous list of no-nos for passengers before take-off. "I'm sorry, sir, I'll have to take your camera out of the overhead rack and ask you to hold it or put it under your seat. Only hats and coats in the overhead rack."

"Why?"

"It is an FAA regulation for your own safety."

"Why?"

"Because it might fall out and hit your head."

"Why?"

And so on.

Like the airlines, stewardesses are reluctant to bring up the possibility of emergencies and danger on an airplane, where the emotional atmosphere is already one of apprehension as far as most passengers are concerned. Unpleasant encounters over regulations with an obstreperous passenger can have a very bad effect on the many cooperative passengers around him. And specific instructions in air safety before take-off tend to scare many passengers half to death. I've often wished news media would shoulder more of the responsibility in informing the public about their responsibilities as passengers in the security of their own homes. There is so much constructive information which passengers could digest while firmly rooted to the ground to reduce their fear of flying and make themselves and their fellow passengers a lot safer in the air. But information on preventive measures to ensure air safety is unfortunately still a taboo subject for the general public.

The fact remains that every time an airplane crashes, it will be front-page news—while investigations and reports on over-crowded and inadequate airport facilities, huge increases in the number of commercial and general airplanes flown, and the great need for government aid and public support in constructing new airports is given little attention in the press. These are all essential in the improvement of air safety.

One of the effects of this government and public apathy was the breakdown of the air-traffic control system during the summers of 1968 and 1969. The controllers have my full sympathy in their fight to improve their working conditions and the inadequate equipment with which they work. Their responsibility is certainly as great as the pilots' in air safety.

In June of 1969 my flight waited in line on the runway five and a half hours before taking off for a six-hour flight to Paris. It was boring and tiresome, but the passengers showed amazing patience and very little irritation over the situation. Very few of them had any idea why they were being held up; they were just praying that they would be able to go to Europe that evening. Again, it was not advisable at that time to inform them what implications their predicament had for air safety. More exposure of the real problems on TV and in the other news media would do a lot to improve the situation by applying pressure to the real culprit—a lethargic Congress voting inadequate funds.

Whenever a plane does crash, the main target for the blame is pilot error. There are very few cases where the pilot has been solely responsible for an accident, but the Air Line Pilots Association and every commercial pilot will be the first to admit that, in any crash, theirs is the greatest responsibility: their most important function at the controls of an airplane is to compensate for design failures, maintenance carelessness, and human error. Many passengers are alive today—often at the expense of the lives of the cockpit crews—because of the skill, dedication, and courage of pilots in performing their duties in an emergency.

Assuming any improvements in the conditions of airport and air-traffic control, the main cause of needless fatalities in the event of a crash will still be smoke inhalation and fire, which account for almost all the deaths in landing and take-off crashes. If fire can eventually be controlled, flying will certainly become the safest way to travel. Continual research is being done on low-combustion fuels and more effective types of fire-extinguishing foam for use on runways and even inside the cabin. Ruptureproof fuel tanks are being designed for new airplanes, and fire-resistant and self-extinguishing materials are being used to replace materials in the interiors of old ones.

Of course, these improvements don't affect your responsibilities as a stewardess; they just make you and everybody else a little safer. Every time you board an airplane, you must check all the emergency equipment and mentally go through the duties of your assigned position. Few crashes are forewarned, so your reflexes must be trained for quick action to avoid panic and tragedy. One of the pilots may spring an impromptu quiz on you and supply you with important bits of information about possible malfunctions of emergency equipment—explaining how you can operate it in that event. Improvisation is often necessary in a crash: you must first know your duties and then improvise if necessary. You can't know too much—every piece of new information may be important. And then you have the sometimes impossible chore of making sure your passengers observe the safety regulations and keeping them smiling at the same time. It's all a part of the job, and no girl who has gone through training would deny that it is the most important part.

To end on a reassuring note, I have been flying for seven years, and have never had a serious emergency. Like all stewardesses, I remain interested in improving air safety, but hope I never have to put this valuable knowledge in practice. Happy landings to us all.

7

AIRBORNE AT LAST

Years ago, in the days before jets, a brand-new stewardess boarding her first flight with the usual mixture of excitement and apprehension was warned by the captain to make sure the first officer was on board before she closed the door: he was invariably late. The captain then gave her a list of duties which kept her so busy she never thought to check on the first officer—who, hiding in the cockpit the whole time, climbed down the cockpit hatch to the baggage compartment.

The captain called the stewardess in, demanding to know where the first officer was; near tears, she explained her forgetfulness. The captain softened his tone: because she was new, she would be given another chance.

As the plane pulled into the gate at their first stop, the first officer climbed out the cockpit window, pulled his clothes askew, and was hanging onto an outside support next to the door when the stewardess opened it. Just for a moment it seemed possible to her that he had been out there clinging for his life the whole trip —until she heard the laughter from the crew behind her.

This story is part of airline history, because today's crews would never go to such elaborate lengths to initiate a new girl into the clan. Flying is a much more serious and complicated business now, and the cockpit crews are too busy to use their imagination in this way. Besides, stewardesses in training hear all the stories— few of them would fall for any tricks today.

After the graduation ceremony, new stewardesses aren't given the chance to indulge in daydreams about what flying is going to be like. If you are not assigned to fly out of the city where you are trained, you're put on the first available flight to your new base. Most airlines reserve rooms in airport motels for the girls until they find their own apartments. Some allow up to five days' expense money for these rooms, but then you are on your own. You are given forty-eight hours to get settled before being put on reserve or assigned a flight to work. Orientation classes are scheduled so that you will know how to check in for your flights, fill out the forms, find your mailbox, and obtain any information pertinent to your base.

These details vary from airline to airline, but one point they all manage to drive home right away is how low you are on the seniority list. A new girl can count on having last choice of everything—from the position she works on flights to when she can take her vacation. It really doesn't seem to make much difference at the time, because you're so glad to be out of training and qualified to fly. It doesn't even matter that much *what* your first flight assignments are—you wouldn't know a good trip from a bad one yet. If it's one with a desirable destination for you—so much the better, that's all. All flights present the new stewardess with the same excitement and problems of adjustment.

To give you an idea of a senior flight: you might fly nonstop New York to San Francisco, have twenty-four hours to enjoy yourself in the Golden Gate city, and have a nonstop flight back, for a total flight time of ten hours. You would work this flight perhaps eight times during the month, using up twelve days, eighty hours' flight time. This would mean eighteen days off, a nice layover, and high flight time, which assures a nice check for incentive pay, added to twelve days' expense money. And the long, nonstop flights would mean a leisurely service which you could enjoy as much as the passengers. Definitely a senior flight.

A junior flight might have one or two of those advantages but definitely not all. One of the first flights I held was grimly referred to as the funeral express. It left at midnight from San Francisco and stopped at Los Angeles, Denver, and Chicago (where we got off), continuing on to Washington, D.C., and New York City. Flights on this propeller airplane, less expensive than the jets, could be depended on to include at least three or four distraught passengers who were rushing as fast as their finances would allow to a family funeral on the opposite coast. Even though we flew only as far as Chicago, we were exhausted after two intermediate stops in the middle of the night, and had to sleep for hours there to prepare ourselves to pick up the same flight returning to San Francisco at two o'clock the next morning. There was a spartan service of box lunches and coffee, no liquor to comfort the bereft passengers. Worst of all, when I transferred from San Francisco to New York five months later, the first flight I was assigned was the funeral express to Chicago.

Not many of the major airlines still fly propeller airplanes— we were actually rather fond of those vibrating old hulks with their small seating capacities. With the assurance of never having to fly one again, I can say that sometimes I miss the intimacy of the funeral express, remembering all the sad and funny stories the sleepless passengers would relate.

Let's hope that *your* first flight is a happy one with a friendly, helpful crew—no food shortages or grumpy passengers. Let the weather be fine so that you can see the view if you have time. I hope that passengers smile back when you smile at them, that you don't suffer stage fright when you talk on the PA, don't trip or spill or burn anything, run your stockings, or lose your baggage. I hope that all of your galley equipment works, that you don't have more garbage than you can cope with, that there aren't too many desserts left over if you have a weight problem, and that at least one passenger tells you how pretty you look in your new uniform. There will be plenty of flights to initiate you into your role of trouble shooter. May your first one be trouble-free and fun—because when you get home there may be some grim realities to face.

If you've found an apartment before your first flight, you can consider yourself fortunate. The difficulties to overcome in this respect vary from city to city. New York, true to its reputation, seems to be the most expensive and generally inhospitable to stewardesses: your application for the privilege of paying an astronomical rent is likely to be refused the minute the real estate brokers discover you are a stewardess.

Dogged by the image again—to them we are irresponsible,

noisy, immoral, sure to skip town without paying the rent. Even putting a three months' deposit in their hands won't dispel their doubts. Fortunately, the stewardess office at your base will have a list of the few friendly brokers in the vicinity, and there are always notices posted by girls who have apartments and want roommates. Moving in with someone already set up in an apartment is certainly the least expensive way to begin life in a new city. But then, most girls have formed friendships during training and will prefer to share an apartment with someone they know.

If this is the case and you are lucky enough to come across a reasonable apartment, the next problem is phone service. Some telephone companies feel the same way the real estate brokers do about stewardesses. A fifty-dollar deposit from each girl in the apartment is the usual shakedown. Of course, you can always tell the phone company there is only one girl in the apartment and then divide up the expense of the deposit, adding the extra names to the phone listings after a month or so. This does require some cleverness in convincing the company that no further deposit is needed—for one thing, you'd better deny that your roommates are stewardesses. And even if the ploy works, the girl stuck with the responsibility for the phone bill could also be stuck with paying for her roommates' phone calls.

Since a telephone is an absolute necessity for a stewardess, there is no way of avoiding the problem. The only good thing about it all is that a portion of your telephone bill can be taken off your income tax.

This is happily true of other things besides phone bills—stewardesses are allowed quite a few deductions, among them shoes, girdles, support hose, gloves, hairdressers, make-up, some taxi fares, and any money spent for expenses over the amount provided.

When income tax time comes around, it is certainly worth the money to use one of the accounting firms that specialize in making out stewardesses' returns. They usually put cards in your mailbox at the airport. You may want to ask around and find out how good they are (they're not if someone who used them has had to explain excessive deductions to the government). But they do know what deductions are allowed. I made out my own return the first year I flew, and received sixty dollars back; the next year I used an accountant and got three hundred dollars back. That big check is always very welcome in the spring.

If you haven't established a credit rating before you start flying, you'll probably have trouble obtaining charge accounts as a stewardess. I certainly did. Unknown to credit bureaus because of my two-year stay in Europe, I found it impossible to open accounts at first—I had no credit rating *and* was one of those unreliable airlines stewardesses. Not having charge cards can be a blessing for those who tend to charge first and worry about paying later. (It was just as well for me that I was rejected by the department stores at first.) But for you reasonable girls, considering how much your beginning paychecks are shrunk by uniform deductions, insurance, and taxes, a charge account can make the difference between buying the frying pan *and* the hamburger or having to choose between the two.

Another financial tip: investigate your airline credit union. You can start saving right away for your vacation by having money deducted from your paycheck before you can get your hands on it and spend it. The rate of interest is favorable, and after six months to a year and a half—depending on the airline—you may borrow money from the credit union at a much lower interest rate than banks offer.

It should be obvious from the foregoing that the immediate expenses of setting yourself up in an apartment—deposits (rent, phone, gas, and electricity); transportation to the airport (you can get a discount book of airport bus or limousine tickets, but you pay for several months' worth in advance); incidental uniform expenses (shoes, hose, scarves, gloves)—can add up to quite a large amount. A new stewardess will need to have set aside about three hundred dollars—more if she's based in New York.

Unless you can borrow this money from home, it can be a real problem—and there are few airlines willing to concern themselves with it. Some will advance you up to a hundred dollars on your salary, but most of them consider it your worry. They feel that financial responsibility is an indication of the maturity necessary to all stewardesses, and are not sympathetic to girls who find themselves in hot water over money.

96

For the first six months of flying, you are on probation—which means you can't just relax and forget about all those regulations once you're out of training. Senior stewardesses, on the other hand, sometimes disregard rules and get away with it. Why can't you? Because *you* can be fired for the least infraction, that's why.

During these six months, you will undoubtedly become very familiar with your supervisor. You may be assigned a kind and understanding one—it depends on luck. I have heard a lot of complaints from stewardesses flying for different airlines about their problems with supervisors. But then, supervisors were once stewardesses themselves, and most are aware of the hostility they can generate by using rules and regulations as laws instead of the guidelines they were meant to be. A supervisor who falls into the category of parole officer can certainly impair good work and relationships, but during the six months of probation it's really not wise to concern yourself with such problems. You don't have a union yet—nor will you have established good relations with management—to protect your job in any dispute.

This is a point worth emphasizing, as you may be tempted to question regulations that seem silly (there are plenty to choose from). But although the rules and regulations sometimes change and are always subject to individual interpretation, the individual whose interpretation is going to count is your supervisor's.

The fact is, petty interpretations can be blown all out of proportion if a confrontation is provoked. Take the case of a girl who had worn little gold crosses in her ears ever since she was five years old. No one had objected to them during training; her airline allowed *round* pierced-ear rings, and the fact that hers were crosses hadn't seemed to bother training personnel. When a supervisor at her new base told her she couldn't wear them, she argued that if it had been all right in training, it should be all right now. Caught wearing them two more times, she was called into the office and dismissed. She had one month to go before she would have been off probation and into the union, which would have made it impossible for her to be fired for such a small infraction of the rules.

The plain truth is, while you are in a poor bargaining position it is poor judgment to challenge authority—even on small points. And after all, it's not surprising that airline management feels it has the right to demand your discipline even in the pettiest matters during the probation period. You're being watched and tested on the ever-present yardstick—a flippant, casual, or recalcitrant attitude could indicate that you might start making up your own rules in safety or emergency procedures.

So be forewarned: if being watched, tested, and generally regimented strikes you as hopelessly incompatible with your personality, this career may not be the right one for you. Most girls, however, find the six months of strict surveillance a reasonable length of time to make the important regulations a matter of habit, not discipline.

Eventually you will be settled at your new base. Depending on the number of stewardesses and the rate at which you move up the seniority list, you may hold a flight sequence immediately or be relegated to the reserve list—from a few months to as much as a year. Some airlines have more equitable reserve policies for new girls than others, rotating reserve assignments so that new stewardesses are often able to hold flights their first month of duty. This certainly has the advantage of letting you know when you'll be home and where you will be flying.

Even if they hold a bad trip (in respect to destinations, time off, overtime, expense money, or how tiring it is), most girls would rather know their schedules ahead of time. But should reserve be inevitable, you can console yourself with the thought that you may be assigned to a senior trip and thus have the chance to enjoy a variety of flight assignments. At its best, reserve gives you a sampling of all the trips from your base, which can help you choose intelligently when you *do* have a choice. It can also mean that you fly regularly and can depend on a good expense and overtime check.

Once a month stewardesses are paid for their expenses and are given any overtime or incentive pay for hours flown over the maximum flight hours for base pay. Delta Airlines gives incentive pay for any hours flown over fifty, but the others don't start until sixty-five to seventy-two hours have been flown. The salary structures can be confusing, and in Part II I have tried to give an idea of what your beginning paychecks might be.

Whatever the structure is, expense and overtime checks will be important to your finances—most new stewardesses feel financially pinched and even though their expenses allow them reasonable amounts for meals away from home, having a hamburger instead of spending the four-dollar dinner allotment can mean money left over to pay the rent.

Airlines usually don't provide meals for stewardesses on flights, but that doesn't mean there is never any food for you. To the contrary, girls with weight problems will find all too much food to sample. In any case, leftover plane meals, hamburgers, or, even better, dinner dates should leave you the major portion of those expense checks to pay your bills or save for a vacation.

But, not surprisingly, things don't always work out for the best as far as finances are concerned. The new and impecunious stewardess may find that due to the lack of regular flights, or trips that pay small expense and overtime checks, she feels hopeless about ever saving enough money to take advantage of her travel benefits. Fortunately, there are ways out of this kind of bind.

Since all but one ° of the twelve major airlines in Part II of this book allow stewardesses to hold outside jobs, you might be interested in the part-time employment firms that specialize in handling airline stewardesses.

Two of these services were organized by ex-airline personnel: Hospitality Services, Inc., and Flight 485. Another organization, called Super Girls, relies heavily on stewardesses. The kind of work available is mainly hostessing at conventions, trade shows, and exhibitions, on a strictly nonfraternization basis. Usually the girls are not allowed to mention the name of the airline they work for, or give out their address or phone number, or drink or smoke while on the job. The pay can be up to fifty dollars a day, and twenty-five to thirty dollars for as few as four hours' work.

One girl I know was sent by Flight 485 to Shea Stadium with a group of other stewardesses to hand out publicity for Borden's— during half time, Elsie the Cow herself was to be escorted onto

° Delta Air Lines does *not* approve outside employment, but then its stewardesses are among the best-paid in the industry. Delta also does not have a base in New York City, which is the seat of most stewardesses' financial crises.

the field. She and the other girls were paid thirty dollars for watching a free football game and, as my friend put it, consorting with a cow. Another girl I know was paid twenty dollars for picking up a cake and delivering it to a man at his office. She sang him a touching "Happy Birthday" and went home with a piece of cake and her paycheck.

This part-time working information is offered simply as a gentle reminder that crying over your poverty will only get you more in debt: something can be done about it even if you don't type, take shorthand, teach, or nurse.

If you're determined not to work outside of flying, and if you aren't already flying your maximum hours, there are ways of increasing your overtime which can bring in a great deal of extra money each month. I worked with a girl on a charter flight to Puerto Rico who increased her overtime and expense money any time she wanted to by bidding long trips which had five to nine days off in between—and then signing up for short charter flights on her days off. Charter flights are becoming more and more popular, and every airline is fighting for its share of the business. Union contracts and working agreements usually specify that these flights be posted ahead of time so that stewardesses can sign up for them. They are awarded on the basis of seniority, but junior stewardesses can usually hold them.

Charter flights can also be frequent assignments for girls on reserve if not enough stewardesses have signed up for them. These flights, I should say, can differ radically from regular commercial flights, depending on the service involved and the amount of liquor consumed. The bar is usually open, meaning the price of liquor is included in the passenger's ticket. The passengers, who are likely to be good drinking buddies before they even board the flight, are consequently likely to be full of festive spirit or spirits. If this is the case, a smooth service according to the book is hopeless. The passengers clog the aisles—singing, drinking, gambling, determined to have a rollicking good time. If you think you're going to be able to control the situation, forget it.

There are ways, though, to swing with it and make it work for you. My first charter flight gave me a planeload of happy salesmen and their wives who had won a trip to Puerto Rico from their

100

company, all expenses paid. They were delirious when they boarded the airplane. The front of the airplane was to be worked by two girls who turned out to be obsessed with imposing the prescribed service on the passengers in an orderly manner, whether they wanted it or not.

I was in the back of the plane with two stewardesses who had seen it all before. We managed to keep the passengers in their seats for dinner, but they were up before we had even begun to collect the trays, shouting for drinks. I muttered under my breath until my mates told me to relax and watch them. Since we couldn't get up or down the aisle, we just drafted the cheerful drinkers to pass us the trays. (It took a little longer than usual, but there was no need to rush on a five-hour flight.) They insisted on making their own drinks, so we set the bar up for them and let them take over. They said sit down and relax, so we sat down and talked with them. Meanwhile more and more people gravitated to the back—the stewardesses up front, serving by the book, were spoiling the passengers' fun.

After a while we made a deal with the busiest bartender: he'd have full charge of the bar, but when we had to serve breakfast, he would make everyone sit down. It all worked like a charm. The passengers had their fun, and we were actually able to enjoy their high spirits. They in turn took care of each other—all the while sympathetically telling us how hard the job must be—and cooperated when the bartender ordered them to sit down.

We arrived in Puerto Rico in reasonably good shape; not surprisingly, the two disciplinarians from the front were exhausted and irritable. I considered that charter flight a lesson learned: let the passengers have a good time, enlist the aid of the most energetic ones, and the service will take care of itself, so to speak.

Most of the time, though, you'll be working noncharter flights —and therefore be at the mercy of Scheduling. New stewardesses should make a point of knowing their union contract or working agreement—it can protect you in dealing with that faceless man from Scheduling who wakes you up and tells you to be at the airport in an hour for a flight. Nice ones will give you a choice of flights, or tell you what your chances are of going out soon, or heed an appeal to assign you a flight to a particular city. But just as often a harried scheduler will frustrate all your plans, deny any requests, and, if you let him, take advantage of your inexperience and send you out on a flight before you've had your legal rest.

This is where knowing what's legal and what isn't is important. Even during probation, Scheduling should observe the same regulations in assigning *your* flight as everyone else's. Granted, the regulations are complicated and often subject to varying interpretations. But if you think you are being treated unfairly, your union representative can advise you even though you aren't yet a member. There are many gray areas that can be clarified, thus saving you unnecessary tears if you are indeed being mistreated. Of course, you should always be sure of legal ground for complaint before involving your supervisor in any disputes with Scheduling.

It's a good idea to be aware of what your union can do for you from the beginning. Unfortunately, union officials for stewardesses have a frustrating job: it is an almost impossible task to gather enough support for a strong bargaining position among a constantly changing list of members, most of whom are young and not aware of how much better their job could be if there were more solidarity among the ranks. New girls may complain how small that beginning paycheck is, but they seldom realize that their lack of interest in their union ensures that the paycheck won't increase much after the next contract is negotiated.

What with the never-ending expenses of expansion and new equipment, airlines are in constant financial crisis. When they have to comply with the demands of the strong unions—such as the pilots and mechanics unions—which increases costs even more, they are naturally prone to try and save by refusing the demands of the stewardesses. Stewardess unions are usually dominated by senior girls who volunteer a great deal of their free time to protect the interests of the junior girls, and in this respect they do a commendable job. But they are ill equipped to get the best of the army of legal and economic experts the company employs to negotiate its side of the contracts. Just remember: your union support is directly related to your financial and working conditions.

If you are lucky enough to avoid any or all of the new-stewardess problems discussed in this chapter, you may nonetheless at times encounter a worse one—loneliness. This isn't a frequent complaint among stewardesses because as a group they tend to be outgoing and to make friends easily. But like all other women, stewardesses go through periods when there's no man around, no friends in the city they're flying to, or no particularly compatible crew members on the flights they're working at the time.

I have suggested antidotes to these possible depressions throughout this book. Here, I'd simply like to offer some ideas to new stewardesses based in a strange city who find they're not coming up with enough friends—specifically, men—and who may be reluctant to dive into the "swinging singles" bars.

This career gives you plenty of time; take advantage of it. Start visiting the art galleries and museums—you don't have to be an art buff to benefit from these places, heavily frequented by men. If you're a part-time student interested in pursuing men along with your studies, do your homework in the pleasant cafes at every college and university. And you don't have to need money to benefit from part-time work. Any job will bring you a whole new group of people to get to know. If you want to meet doctors, do volunteer work in hospitals. The point is, flying makes it easier to *do* something about the problem of loneliness than any career I can think of.

All my warnings and advice, I should say, are meant to be assimilated and filed away in your mind along with the hope that you will have no cause to use them. Much of my knowledge about real problems has come second-hand from other girls' experiences, because in seven years of flying I have had to deal with only a few of them.

I can only hope that your flying career will be as trouble-free as mine has been: I wrote this book because I really do enjoy my job for all the reasons I've included, and I hope that a lot of other young women will find these reasons convincing enough to at least consider this career. At its best, flying can offer most girls a uniquely flexible and mobile way of life. At the least, it offers a definite, interesting thing to do for a few years after school or college.

Be careful, though. There are insidious tendencies to regimentation which can creep into your life subliminally when your uniform is in the closet, as an experience of mine illustrates all too well: Soon after I began flying international routes, I gave a very special dinner party. While my guests sipped away at their coffee, I arranged an impressive array of duty-free liquors and glasses on my serving cart and went zipping into the living room with it, offering after-dinner drinks all around.

My guests were stunned into silence at my razzle-dazzle, clink-clank entrance. One finally whispered, "It's just like an airplane," and asked me gently, "Do you always do this?" I had apparently succeeded in reducing my living room to an airplane aisle—obviously, my job was beginning to brainwash me.

I managed to get a grip on myself and avoid installing seat belts on my easy chairs. But from time to time I do recall the warning of that great individualist Thoreau: "Beware of all enterprises that require new clothes."

PART II

The
Airlines

Specific information on the twelve major U.S. flag carriers is included in Part II. General points to keep in mind when choosing an airline are:

Where do you want to fly? Examine the routes of each airline to see which ones appeal to you the most.

Where do you want to live? Examine the base cities and the number of stewardesses at each base. The bases with the highest number of girls are usually the ones available to new stewardesses. You may check this information at your interview. An even better way is to ask a stewardess already working for the airline which are the junior and senior bases.

Do you meet the general requirements? If there is one requirement which you don't meet but think you might be able to talk your way around in the interview, give the airline a try. You have nothing to lose, and you may be so extraordinary that an exception will be made in your case.

How are the fringe benefits in view of your interests? If you want to continue your studies, check to see if the airline has any educational aid program. It could save you a lot of money, and indicates that the airline is sympathetic to this endeavor. If you are already planning your personal travel, pay special attention to the reduced-rate and pass-privilege information.

What about the uniform? It seems foolish to choose or reject an airline for its uniform designs, but it happens all the time. Be warned that uniforms are now sometimes changed as frequently as every year; you could start out with one you love and then have it changed to one you hate to put on. Once you start flying, you'll find that the design can seem less important than how easy it is to maintain—a drip-dry uniform can save you hundreds of dollars in dry-cleaning bills or tedious hours of ironing.

Will the salary be good? Some of the salary scales quoted in Part II will have changed by the time this book is published, although I have tried to include changes resulting from recent contract negotiations. In general, contracts are renegotiated every two years. You will see that some airlines have much higher pay scales than others, but new contracts have meant that some of the airlines who paid the lowest salaries when I began flying now pay the highest.

Another consideration in evaluating the salary scale is the base cities to which you are likely to be assigned as a new stewardess. New York, Chicago, Los Angeles, and San Francisco have a much higher cost of living than other base cities—you'd better first consider an airline now paying one of the higher salaries if you hope to live in one of them.

Stewardesses generally receive incentive pay and expenses a month after they have earned them—which means you can't expect any of the average paychecks included in Part II until your second month of flying. And the average monthly income I have computed could be more or could be less. To see how much *less* it could be, just subtract the incentive pay and half of the expenses. You will then understand how difficult it is for those new stewardesses who aren't assigned enough flights to make ends meet.

8

AMERICAN AIRLINES

American Airlines, which flies the United States, Mexico, and the near Pacific, employs about 4000 stewardesses and estimates that it trains 1500 each year. As its projection for the next five years calls for an increase to 9000 stewardesses, American is expanding its already lavish training facilities.

QUALIFICATIONS

Age: 20 minimum. Girls may apply at 19½ for assignment to future classes.

Height: 5'2" to 5'9".

Weight: 100 to 140 pounds, in proportion to height, using American's guidelines.

Vision: Uncorrected vision to 20/50 is acceptable. If contact lenses are worn, uncorrected vision must be at worst 20/100 in one eye and 20/200 in the other. When lenses are worn, there must be no signs of irritation for at least ten hours a day.

Marital status: Single at time of employment. Childless widows and divorcees will be considered. (Divorcees should have final divorce papers to show at interview.) Stewardesses may marry and keep flying after completing the six-month probationary period.

Education: High school graduate; college or working experience preferred.

Language: English (girls wishing to fly Mexican routes should also speak Spanish).

Citizenship: United States citizen or alien with a permanent visa.

Health: Must pass American's physical examination.

109

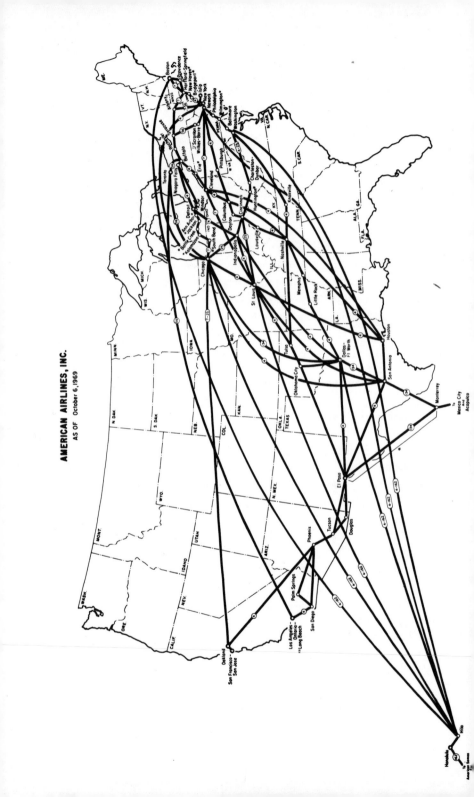

AMERICAN AIRLINES, INC.

AS OF October 6, 1969

TRAINING

American was the first airline to build a separate Stewardess Training College, of which it is justifiably very proud. The college is located halfway between Dallas and Fort Worth on forty-seven acres of rolling hills. Girls accepted by American are flown at the company's expense to the college for a six-week training period. They share a room with three other girls and have the use of all facilities, including tennis courts and bicycles for their free time. American is rather strict about observation of dormitory rules. The school is some distance from Dallas and Fort Worth, so excursions to these cities are limited mainly to the weekends. American spares no expense in training equipment and instructors, and its stewardesses receive some of the best training in the industry.

American maintains a strong sorority atmosphere at the school, which instills a great amount of enthusiasm in its stewardesses. Graduation ceremonies there leave hardly a dry eye in the house. Families and friends are invited, and American gives a buffet luncheon afterward complete with champagne and songs.

Because American provides everything during training—meals, housing, even a heated swimming pool—girls need only bring incidental expense money with them. The airline suggests they also have $300 in reserve to cover personal expenses after graduation at their base cities until the first paycheck is received.

UNION

American stewardesses are affiliated with ALSSA, membership in which is mandatory after the six-month probation period. The initiation fee is $10, and dues are deducted from each semimonthly paycheck at the rate of $2.25.

UNIFORMS

American presently has a washable, drip-dry uniform (skirt and vest) in a selection of colors: red, blue, and the required Ameri-clan plaid, worn with a white blouse and optional ascot—with or without ruffle. The individual items are priced as follows:

Vest and one skirt, Ameri-clan plaid	$ 37.00
Vest and one skirt, choice of red or blue	37.00
Coat, Ameri-clan plaid with interliner and cape	50.00
Blouse:	14.00
Ruffled ascot	4.85
Ascot (without ruffle)	4.50
Purse	13.80
Smock	7.85
	$169.00

Optional:

Davy Crockett fur hat	7.65

Payment for these items is deducted from each semimonthly paycheck in the amount of $10. Boots are given and uniform shoes are available in various price ranges (if you have easy-to-fit feet, you can pay as little as $20). At the end of training, American gives each girl $100 for relocating expenses. Part of this money may be used for buying the uniform suitcase ($23), gloves, scarf, and shoes. After the initial uniform expense is deducted from paychecks (which takes almost two years), American provides all new uniform items at its expense.

SALARY

Monthly base pay up to 71 hours' flying time:

First six months	$420.00
Six months to one year	450.00
Second year	475.00
increasing to	
Maximum after 9 years	660.00

Incentive pay for each hour flown over 71 to maximum of 77 hours per month:

First six months	$ 6.80
Six months to one year	7.29
Second year	7.69
increasing to	
Ninth year	10.69

Expense money

Breakfast	$ 1.92
Lunch	2.20
Dinner	4.75
Midnight snack	1.65
Taxi fare for any flight leaving after 10 P.M. and before 7 A.M. and arriving after 9 P.M. and before 6 A.M.	2.25

American's stewardesses are paid on the 15th and 30th of each month. Expense money and incentive pay are included on the last-of-the-month paycheck only. To give you a rough idea of what a new stewardess can expect to receive from her paychecks after deductions, let's assume you've flown 77 hours during this particular month. Six hours of incentive pay plus, say, $50 expense money would come to you on your last paycheck of the month. I have deducted a straight 20 percent for taxes; this amount could vary by a few dollars according to state tax and the exemptions or deductions on your income tax deduction form.

15th-of-month paycheck

$210 minus	$42.00	taxes		
	10.00	uniform		
	$52.00		$158.00	net pay

30th-of-month paycheck

$210 plus	$40.20	incentive pay		
	50.00	expenses		
	$90.20			
minus	$60.05	taxes		
	10.00	uniform		
	$70.05		$230.15	net pay

The second paycheck would probably be considered good for a girl in her first six months. There is no guarantee that you will be flying over 71 hours or that your trips will bring you that much expense money. American stewardesses tell me the expense checks can be as low as $30 and sometimes go as high as $100, depending on the flights worked.

FRINGE BENEFITS

Stewardesses receive two weeks' paid vacation after a year of employment. Vacation passes on American are given *in addition to* the regular pass allotment you receive as an employee of the airline.

Group life, hospitalization, accident, and health insurance premiums are paid by American. Additional insurance is available at reasonable rates if desired.

American does not offer any educational aid to its stewardesses.

RESERVE POLICY

New stewardesses can expect to be on reserve one month out of four. While on reserve you are assured five 48-hour periods a month when you're not on call. You are assigned a bid immediately after graduation. The second month you are on reserve—and every fourth month thereafter until you are senior enough to hold a bid regularly.

TRAVEL BENEFITS

New stewardesses are eligible for reduced rates (50 to 75 percent discounts on American and other airlines) after six months of employment.

Passes are allotted as follows:

Six months to one year: two round-trip passes or 3000 miles.

One to two years: four round-trip passes or 5000 miles, with passes and mileage increasing with each year of employment. American has reciprocal pass agreements with some other airlines.

All vacation passes are in addition to this pass allowance. American stewardesses are also allowed vacation passes for both parents; one brother, one sister, or husband; and dependent children. (This means stepchildren, since American stewardesses are not allowed to continue flying after having children.)

BASE CITIES

	APPROXIMATE NO. OF STEWARDESSES
Boston	300
Washington, D.C.	150
Buffalo	150
Nashville	120
Dallas	550
New York	1000
Chicago	650
Los Angeles	700
San Francisco	300

The cities with the highest number of girls are likely bases for new stewardesses, with New York one of the most probable. But a small base like Buffalo, which might not sound very exciting, is another possibility for new and therefore junior girls. Bases are assigned to each graduating class according to age, oldest girls getting first choice of the openings.

You may request a transfer to any base, subject to openings and seniority, after the first six months of employment. American claims to have stewardess turnover of nearly 100 percent every two years, which means its girls must climb the seniority list rapidly. You are only as junior as the number of girls in front of you.

MISCELLANEOUS

American's stewardesses participate in the Thomas Dooley Foundation (see page 33).

Special assignments are offered to stewardesses for promotion and public relations on a voluntary basis. The pay is $10 a day plus expenses.

American allows its stewardesses to hold outside jobs subject to supervisory approval.

American has a unique plan for inducing its stewardesses to retire at thirty-two. Girls are called into the office when they reach 31½ and offered a contract to sign which will bring them $250 for every year they've been employed by American if they will retire before their thirty-third birthday. Once signed, this contract is irrevocable, but there is no pressure put on stewardesses to sign it. A married friend of mine who flies for American is looking forward to collecting $2000 on her thirty-third birthday and retiring to raise a family.

WHERE TO APPLY

Application forms may be obtained by writing to:

Manager, Stewardess Recruitment
AMERICAN AIRLINES, INC.
3300 West Mocking Bird Lane
Dallas, Texas 75235

9

BRANIFF INTERNATIONAL AIRLINES

Braniff employs about 1500 stewardesses flying the United States, Latin America, and military charters to the Far East and Europe. Stewardesses who fly the military charters are based at Travis Air Force Base, outside San Francisco. Braniff has a Latin American division with a separate stewardess corps made up of girls from these countries. American-based girls do not fly farther south than Mexico, although all of Braniff's commercial routes are available to them on passes and at reduced rates.

QUALIFICATIONS

Age: 19½ minimum at time of employment.

Height: 5'2" to 5'9".

Weight: 105 to 135 pounds.

Vision: Uncorrected vision must be at least 20/50; 20/100 if contact lenses are worn.

Marital status: Single girls, childless widows and divorcees are accepted. You may marry and keep flying after completing probation.

Education: High school graduates; college or working experience preferred.

Language: Spanish, Chinese, or Japanese is preferred in addition to English.

Citizenship: United States citizen or permanent visa.

Health: Must pass a physical examination.

BRANIFF INTERNATIONAL

U.S. MAINLAND   HAWAII   MEXICO   SOUTH AMERICA

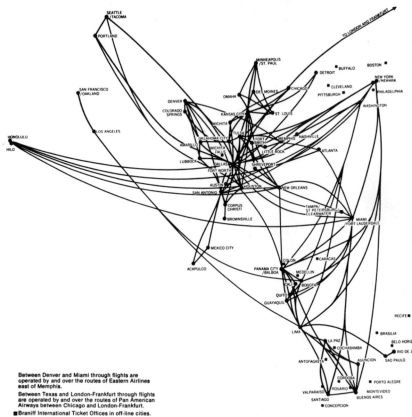

Between Denver and Miami through flights are
operated by and over the routes of Eastern Airlines
east of Memphis.

Between Texas and London-Frankfurt through flights
are operated by and over the routes of Pan American
Airways between Chicago and London-Frankfurt.

■ Braniff International Ticket Offices in off-line cities.

A quality company of Ling-Temco-Vought, Inc. **LTV**

TRAINING

In 1968 Braniff opened a two-million-dollar International Hostess Training College, which is the prettiest and most compact training school I have visited. It is a modern high-rise building situated in a residential area of Dallas. The décor reflects the airline's routes —vibrant colors and Latin American folk art decorate every room. It is the most personal institutional building I have ever been in (every bedroom has a different color scheme, with Mexican bedspreads and art on the walls). The building has all the luxuries of an expensive beauty spa: heated swimming pool, beauty salon, game room complete with a pool table for dates, color television, a 40-foot-square mirrored exercise room with sinister-looking contraptions to push and bump you into shape, plus a sauna that accommodates twelve people, and bathrooms in black marble throughout.

Braniff transports its trainees to Dallas for a five-week program. Everything is provided during training (make-up, room and board, hair styling, cab fares, and even the first visit to a dermatologist), so incidental expense money is all you need. Because Braniff doesn't have bases in cities with an exorbitant cost of living, it suggests that girls have a minimum of only $150 to cover expenses after training until their first paycheck.

Dormitory rules are liberal on weekends, and dates may be entertained in the game rooms and lounges throughout the week in the afternoon and evening (should you have the time). Graduation is celebrated with a champagne luncheon.

Braniff will give a generous advance of $250 to new stewardesses to help them get settled. This money is deducted from their future paychecks.

Since all expenses are paid by Braniff (although it does suggest you bring $100 for incidental expenses during training), girls can safely begin a career with Braniff with less than the savings recommended by most of the other major airlines.

UNION

Membership is not mandatory, but hostesses may join ALPA after the six-month probation period has been completed. The dues are $4.50 per month.

UNIFORMS

Braniff was the first airline to introduce high fashion into uniform design. Emilio Pucci has designed basic dresses in pink and plum Trevira to be worn with a Pucci scarf, panty hose, and shoes matched to the color of the dress. The dresses are washable and drip-dry. A coat, smock, and boots complete this outfit.

There are no details available for prices of individual uniform items, but the initial cost to new stewardesses is $240, and is paid for by a $15 deduction from each paycheck. Replacements following a reasonable period of wear are paid for by the company.

SALARY

Monthly base pay for 70 hours' flight time

First six months	$355.00
Six months to one year	370.00
Second year	385.00
increasing to	
Nine years	550.00

Incentive pay for each hour flown over 70

Per hour	$ 10.00

Expense money

Breakfast	$ 1.50
Lunch	1.75
Dinner	3.75
Midnight snack	1.50

Paychecks are received on the 5th and 20th of every month, including base and incentive pay. Expense checks arrive on the 1st and 15th.

Each girl flies an average of 80 to 85 hours per month. A new stewardess flying 80 hours (70 hours' pay and 10 hours' incentive pay) might receive a paycheck like this:

5th-of-the-month paycheck (base pay plus incentive)

$227.50 minus	$45.50 taxes	
	15.00 uniform	
	$60.50	$167.00 net pay

1st-of-the-month expense check

$50.00

2.50 cleaning expense

$52.50

The 20th-of-the-month paycheck and 15th-of-the-month expense check would presumably be the same, giving a monthly net income of $438.

FRINGE BENEFITS

Stewardesses receive two weeks' paid vacation from one through seven years of employment.

Braniff has an insurance program for its employees, and pays 100 percent of the premiums for accident, health, medical, and surgical policies.

Braniff does not offer educational aid to its stewardesses.

RESERVE POLICY

New stewardesses are on reserve until they have enough seniority to hold a flight. This can be within the first few months of flying.

TRAVEL BENEFITS

At the end of six months' service a hostess receives one Braniff pass. At the end of the first year of employment, unlimited passes with a fee of $6 for coach and $12 for first class are issued. These may be used at any time, including vacation, without other restrictions. Husbands and parents are also eligible to use any of the allotted passes. One non-Braniff pass is permitted per year, to be used during vacation.

Braniff has reduced-rate agreements with most domestic and international airlines, the discounts ranging from 50 to 75 percent.

BASE CITIES

	NO. OF STEWARDESSES
Dallas	640
Kansas City, Mo.	83

Minneapolis	75
Travis Air Force Base, Calif	
(military flights)	165
Houston	80

Braniff considers a girl's preference when making base assignments, but final decisions are subject to available openings. When trainees graduate from hostess college, age determines seniority, with the oldest girl having first choice of base assignment.

MISCELLANEOUS

Braniff participates in the Thomas Dooley Foundation program.

The company allows stewardesses to hold outside jobs subject to supervisory approval.

Braniff requires its hostesses to appear in promotional and non-flight assignments. The girls are paid for these, but the rate varies with the type of special assignment.

WHERE TO APPLY

Application forms may be obtained by writing to:

> Manager of Hostess Employment
> BRANIFF BUILDING
> Exchange Park
> Dallas, Texas 75235

or from Braniff airport counters and ticket offices. Personal application may be made at the Dallas office. Braniff calls in qualified applicants for a personal interview, or notifies them of an interview to be given in their area. The average time between application and acceptance is three weeks.

10

CONTINENTAL AIRLINES

Continental currently employs 1000 stewardesses, and this number is expanding very rapidly.

This company feels that since its stewardesses have the most contact with the passengers, they should be held responsible for carrying out all efforts for good service. Applicants should project an attitude of caring for the passengers' needs and should seem enthusiastic about fulfilling them. Volunteer work in hospitals or charitable organizations is therefore good experience to have if applying to Continental—Continental feels that it helps produce the attitude it looks for when hiring stewardesses.

QUALIFICATIONS

Age: The minimum is 20.

Height: 5'3" to 5'9".

Weight: 140 pounds maximum, in proportion to height.

Vision: 20/50 vision is the minimum; 20/100 if corrected to 20/50 for applicants with contact lenses. The latter must have been wearing contacts successfully prior to acceptance.

Marital status: Single, divorced, or widowed, with no children.

Education: High school graduate.

Citizenship: United States citizen, or permanent alien resident.

TRAINING

Continental's training school is located in a well-equipped, modern training center on the fringe of the Los Angeles Airport.

CONTINENTAL AIRLINES
DOMESTIC ROUTES

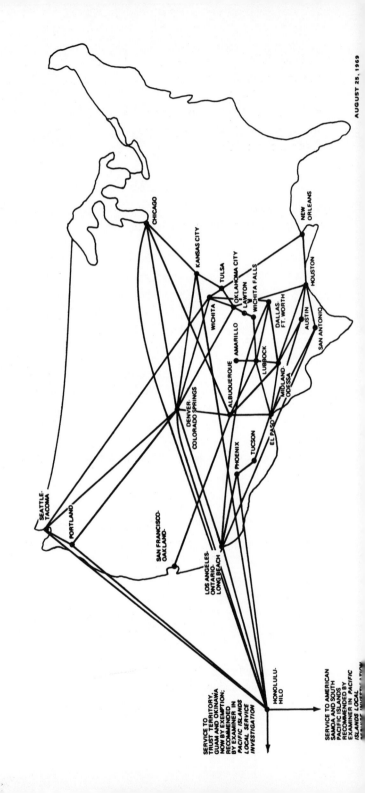

SERVICE TO
TRUST TERRITORY,
GUAM AND OKINAWA
NOW BY EXEMPTION;
RECOMMENDED
BY EXAMINER IN
PACIFIC ISLANDS
LOCAL SERVICE
INVESTIGATION

SERVICE TO AMERICAN
SAMOA AND SOUTH
PACIFIC ISLANDS
RECOMMENDED BY
EXAMINER IN PACIFIC
ISLANDS LOCAL
SERVICE INVESTIGATION

AUGUST 25, 1969

CHICAGO

KANSAS CITY

TULSA

WICHITA

OKLAHOMA CITY

LAWTON

WICHITA FALLS

AMARILLO

DALLAS-
FT. WORTH

ALBUQUERQUE

LUBBOCK

AUSTIN

MIDLAND-
ODESSA

SAN ANTONIO

DENVER-
COLORADO SPRINGS

HOUSTON

NEW
ORLEANS

PHOENIX

TUCSON

EL PASO

SEATTLE-
TACOMA

PORTLAND

SAN FRANCISCO-
OAKLAND

LOS ANGELES-
ONTARIO-
LONG BEACH

HONOLULU-
HILO

Trainees are housed at the Hacienda Motel nearby. The company provides transportation to the school and pays for the trainee's room. Training lasts five weeks, during which the girls receive $4 per day expense money. Continental advises each girl to bring approximately $200 to cover personal needs until the first regular paycheck is received.

UNION

Continental's stewardesses are affiliated with ALPA; membership is voluntary. There is no initiation fee, and dues are $54 per year.

UNIFORMS

New stewardesses pay $160 for winter and $95.35 for summer uniforms, on a salary-deduction plan ($20 per month) if desired. The company makes replacements for all items when needed due to wear or a change in design.

Continental's stewardess wardrobe presently consists of a black serge dress and jacket with double-row brass buttons for winter. A red velour beret and red patent hatbox complete the ensemble.

The summer uniform is a pink Dacron cord dress and jacket worn with a white straw beret and black patent hatbox. The shoes for both uniforms are black pumps with Pilgrim buckles.

SALARY

Monthly base pay for 65 hours' flight time

First six months	$380
Six months to one year	405
Second year	425
usual increase to	
Nine years	565

Domestic incentive pay for each hour flown over 65:

Jet aircraft	$ 11.00
Propeller aircraft	8.50

International: in addition to incentive pay, hourly payment is made for international flight time at the rate of $1.55 per hour flown.

Expenses: Stewardesses are reimbursed for expenses at the following rates for each hour or fraction thereof, from the time they report for duty until termination of flight:

> *Domestic*
> 40¢ per hour first 10 hours,
> 45¢ thereafter
> *International*
> 45¢ per hour

A stewardess flying 70 hours one month on jet aircraft (5 hours' incentive pay) might have a net monthly income of:

Net base pay	$282.00	(taxes, uniform, and insurance deducted)
Net incentive pay	44.00	
Expenses	80.00	
Total net income	$406.00	

FRINGE BENEFITS

A stewardess is eligible for her first vacation with Continental in the next calendar year following her employment. Vacation is accrued at the rate of 1.2 days per month of service; three weeks after 12 years.

Group life insurance is available, with the employee paying the premiums. Hospitalization and accident and health insurance are paid for by the company.

RESERVE POLICY

New stewardesses are on reserve until they have enough seniority to hold a flight. This can be within the first few months of flying.

TRAVEL BENEFITS

Stewardesses are eligible for reduced-rate transportation on Continental immediately upon employment; after six months of service, you receive reduced-rate privileges on certain other airlines. The number and frequency of passes increases with seniority. Parents and husbands are also eligible for travel privileges, and your vacation transportation is in addition to the regular pass allowance.

BASE CITIES

	APPROX. NO. OF STEWARDESSES
Los Angeles	496
Denver	120
Seattle	76
Dallas	86
Houston	46
Guam	14

Continental assignments depend on company needs, but the chances of a new graduate's being based in the location she chooses are good. You may request a transfer to another base any time after your first assignment.

Age dictates seniority in determining which girls in a new graduating class have their choice of base assignments.

MISCELLANEOUS

Stewardesses are not allowed to take outside paying jobs without prior written permission from the company. Not surprisingly, charitable volunteer work is permitted.

WHERE TO APPLY

Application forms may be obtained by writing to:

> Personal Relations Division
> CONTINENTAL AIRLINES, INC.
> Los Angeles International Airport
> Los Angeles, California

or from local ticket and airport offices. Personal application may be made at the Los Angeles and Denver offices.

If a girl meets the basic requirements as stated on the application, Continental furnishes her with a trip pass to Los Angeles for interviews. Final acceptance notice is contingent upon schedule of future class dates. Once accepted, a girl will report for training in three weeks.

11

DELTA AIR LINES

Delta, although a major United States flag carrier with coast-to-coast routes, is a Southern airline at heart. Its headquarters are in Atlanta, Georgia, and it seems steeped in the tradition of Southern hospitality without having the antiquated ideas that Northerners may associate with the South.

Delta views its stewardesses as ladies, first and foremost. It does not accept divorcees. Uniform hems are presently a discreet one inch above the knee. Outside employment is not allowed, the implication perhaps being that a Delta stewardess with time on her hands would devote it to charitable endeavors. She wouldn't need the extra money, anyway—Delta has been a forerunner in good working conditions and high salaries. It has in fact been so successful in keeping its stewardesses happy that it is the only major airline that is nonunionized. Delta's gentleman's agreement with its ladies is enviable.

Delta presently employs over 2000 stewardesses.

QUALIFICATIONS

Age: 20 to 27.

Height: 5'2" to 5'8".

Weight: 113 to 140 pounds, in proportion to height (an increase of one or two pounds is allowed for each additional inch in height).

Vision: Uncorrected vision of at least 20/100 with no astigmatism. Contact lenses are permitted if applicant has been wearing them successfully for six months.

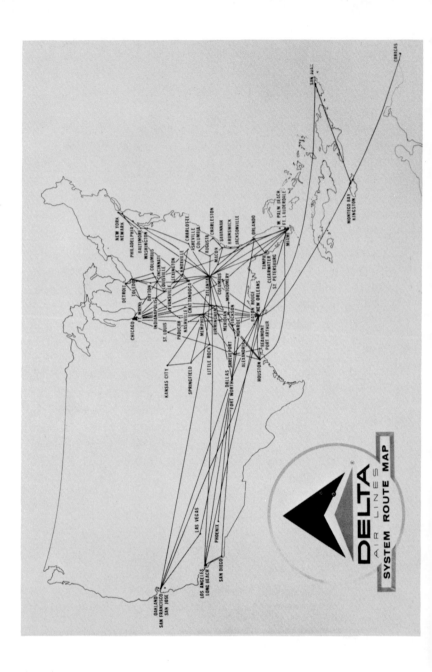

DELTA
AIR LINES
SYSTEM ROUTE MAP

Marital status: Single (never married). Stewardesses who have completed the six-month probation period may marry and continue flying.

Education: High school graduate with two years of college or business experience.

Language: None required for employment, but ability to speak Spanish is an asset and is required for international flying.

Citizenship: U.S. citizen.

Health: Must be able to pass Delta's physical examination.

TRAINING

Delta's training school is part of a ground training center located just off Atlanta Airport. It is a high-rise apartment office building with classrooms, housing quarters, and a swimming pool for the trainees. The dormitory is well supplied with laundry rooms, lounges, professional hair dryers, and maid service. Delta has an arrangement with a nearby cafeteria, which supplies meals. Dormitory hours are strict, and no dating is allowed during the week.

The length of the training period is four and a half weeks. Girls are advised to bring money to cover personal expenses until the first paycheck is received. A new Delta stewardess based in Atlanta told me that it cost her $200 to settle in an apartment before she received her paycheck.

It may not be the most glamorous of the new training schools, but it does have one of the friendliest atmospheres. The instructors are lively and concerned with the trainees, determined to bring them through successfully. And as I have said, the South can have a lot of charm.

UNION

Delta's stewardesses are not affiliated with any union.

UNIFORMS

Summer
    2 knit dresses, choice of
        pastel (blue, green, or
        yellow) $ 47.00

Belt	2.00
Purse	20.00
Tunic	8.50
Scarf	2.00
Raincoat (beige)	36.20
	$115.70

Winter

Two dresses, one black with jacket, one red	$ 56.60
Beret (red and black)	11.50
Belt	1.20
Tunic	8.50
Raincoat	36.35
Winter coat	67.85
	$182.00

Delta requires new stewardesses to buy the first season's uniform, deducted from their pay at $7.50 per check. The next season's uniform is provided by Delta. Any replacements are paid for by the stewardess.

SALARY

During the first six months, Delta pays a flat salary of $500 a month. This assures new girls of a dependable income no matter how few hours they fly on reserve. After six months they will have enough seniority to hold a bid. Stewardesses fly between 80 and 85 hours a month.

After six months, you receive a monthly base pay for every 50 hours of flying time.

Monthly base pay	
Six months to a year	$425
Second year	445
annual increases to	
Ninth year	530

Incentive pay (called flight pay) for each hour flown over 50 hours per month:

Six months to a year	$5.95
One year to five years	6.00

International flight pay: an additional $1 for each hour flown.

Taxi money: paid during certain hours.

Expenses

Breakfast	$2.00
Lunch	2.25
Dinner	4.25
Midnight snack	2.00

The 15th and the last day of each month are pay days, with paychecks available on Friday if regular paydays fall on weekends or holidays. Incentive pay and expense money are paid on the 15th of each month.

Both paychecks are the same (15th and end of month).

A sample paycheck during the first six months after deductions was given to me by a Delta stewardess:

$250.00 minus

	$39.63 income tax
	12.00 social security
	5.51 state tax
	1.40 insurance—additional
	1.00 credit union
	7.50 uniform
— 67.03	$67.03 total deductions

$182.97 net pay + $40.00 expenses = $222.97

Stewardesses must join the credit union to be issued an airline identification card.

Therefore, for the first six months, a Delta stewardess can expect a monthly net income of $445.94. However, as soon as she has completed her probation, her income can increase considerably because she is then eligible for incentive pay.

FRINGE BENEFITS

A stewardess is eligible for two weeks of paid vacation with Delta after one year of employment. After eight years this increases to three weeks.

Delta has a complete employee insurance program, including group life, hospitalization, and accident, and health. The company pays 100 percent of the premiums.

After six months of service, you may receive educational aid for accredited courses: 75 percent of tuition if you receive grade A; 50 percent for grades B or C. You may also receive up to $50 per course, $200 per calendar year.

RESERVE POLICY

New stewardesses are on reserve until they have enough seniority to hold a flight. This can be within the first few months of flying.

TRAVEL BENEFITS

After 30 days' employment, stewardesses are eligible for reduced rates on Delta. After six months, pass privileges and reduced rates on other airlines are allotted. Passes increase in number with length of service. In addition, there are reciprocal pass arrangements with other airlines.

BASE CITIES

	NO. OF STEWARDESSES
Atlanta	360
Chicago	186
Miami	175
Dallas	209
Houston	200
Memphis	169
New Orleans	216

MISCELLANEOUS

Delta is considering participation in the Thomas Dooley Foundation.

Sometimes Delta requires its stewardesses to appear in promotional and nonflight assignments. Girls are paid $10 per day for these special assignments, plus pay and actual expenses.

WHERE TO APPLY

Application forms may be obtained by writing to:

System Employment Manager
DELTA AIR LINES
Atlanta Airport
Atlanta, Georgia 30320

or from local airport and ticket offices. Except in states where prohibited by law, two recent photos must accompany the completed application, one close-up, one full-length.

Delta will contact girls who meet the basic eligibility requirements for a personal interview, and will provide pass transportation only to Atlanta for out-of-town applicants.

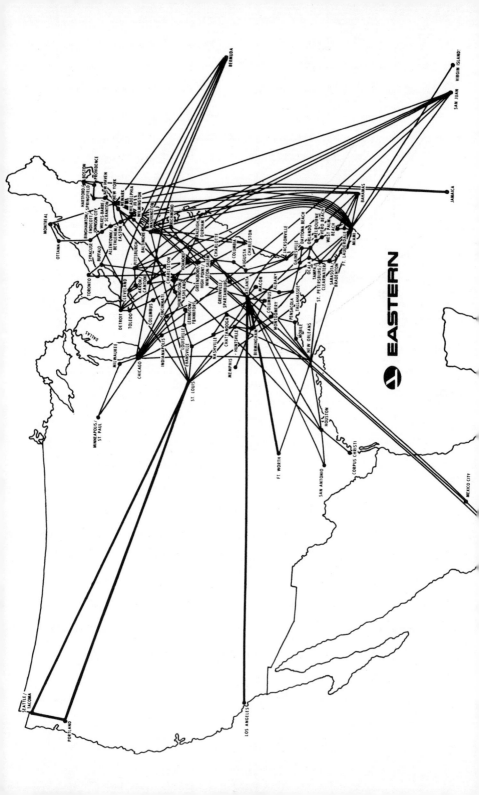

12

EASTERN AIRLINES

Eastern employs approximately 4100 stewardesses and plans to increase this number in the next few years. Servicing mainly the Eastern Seaboard and states, and the eastern half of the Midwest, Eastern also has routes to the West Coast and Canada, and southwest to Mexico, the Bahamas, and Puerto Rico.

Eastern is famous to commuters and frequent travelers for having introduced the shuttle flights, which allow passengers to buy their tickets on board. They continue to be innovators in the industry, as is reflected by some rather advanced training methods for their stewardesses and their extremely liberal pass privileges.

Eastern's headquarters are in New York and Miami, and the training school is in Miami. They look for girls with a "more than average interest in life," and consider a pleasant, outgoing personality essential.

QUALIFICATIONS

Age: 19½ minimum. Actual employment begins at 20, although applications are accepted and processed a half-year earlier.

Height: 5'2" to 5'9".

Weight: 105 to 135 pounds, in proportion to height.

Vision: 20/40 uncorrected in each eye, or 20/200 corrected to 20/40 with contacts.

Marital status: Single; widows and divorcees without children are considered. Stewardesses who marry during employment may continue flying.

Education: High school graduate, although some college is

preferred. Sales experience or public contact work is also welcomed.

Language: No foreign language is required, although Spanish or French are considered desirable.

Citizenship: United States citizen, or alien with permanent visa.

Health: Must pass Eastern's physical examination.

TRAINING

Eastern's training school is located in the Miami Springs Villas, a beautiful old Spanish colonial-style resort hotel with extensive grounds including an Olympic-size swimming pool, tennis courts, and fine restaurants. Eastern's energetic training program leaves girls little time to indulge themselves in the dreamy, romantic atmosphere of the school's setting—tropical gardens, huge shady trees, and pools that are a sanctuary for flamingos and other exotic birds.

Along with the usual training courses, Eastern has been experimenting with "sensitivity training"—a psychologically oriented course in which girls are encouraged to express their feelings about each other and themselves in order to break down barriers of communication. Eastern hopes this experiment will help its stewardesses relate better to the passengers, and feels that so far it has been successful in encouraging the warmth and spontaneity wanted in its stewardesses.

The training period is five weeks, and room and board plus $1 a day incidental expense money are provided by the company. Eastern gives each new graduate $120.80 for relocating expenses, and suggests that she bring $200 for settling expenses after graduation.

UNION

Eastern stewardesses are affiliated with ALSSA; membership is compulsory. The initiation fee is $10; annual dues are $54.

UNIFORMS

Eastern's summer uniform includes knit dresses in six colors from which stewardesses may choose two, a blue trenchcoat, and white accessories. The winter uniform is a navy-blue pants suit, culottes, white knit shirt, and beige coat. Eastern deducts $10 per month from a stewardess's paycheck until payment is completed.

SALARY

Monthly base pay up to 70 hours' flying time:

First six months	$378
Six months to one year	395
Second year	420
increasing annually to	
Eighth year	587

Incentive pay (called flight pay) for each hour flown over 70 hours per month:

Prop-jet junior stewardess		$6.06 per hour
Jet	junior stewardess	6.49 per hour

Expenses: An Eastern stewardess is paid 40¢ per hour expenses for all time spent away from her base, plus additional amounts for layovers over 10 hours.

A new stewardess flying 80 hours on jet equipment (10 hours incentive pay) might have a monthly net income of:

Net base pay	$285.40	(Taxes, uniform and insurance deducted)
Net incentive pay	52.90	
Expenses	120.00	
	$458.30	

FRINGE BENEFITS

After one year of employment, a stewardess is eligible for 15 days of paid vacation. Length of vacation increases depending on years of service with the company.

A group life insurance policy is available at a very low rate, and employees receive company-paid group hospitalization, surgical, and medical insurance. Medical and first-aid centers are available for any minor illnesses or injuries.

Eastern has an educational aid program for its stewardesses.

RESERVE POLICY

New stewardesses are on reserve until they have enough seniority to hold a flight. This can be within the first few months of flying.

TRAVEL BENEFITS

You are eligible for half-fare benefits on Eastern after three months of employment; after six months' service you receive unlimited air travel for yourself and parents for a small service charge. Travel privileges when flying Eastern are unrestricted as to frequency and mileage for eligible employees, their parents and dependents.

Reduced rates are available on other airlines with whom Eastern has interline agreements, and some airlines have reciprocal pass agreements with Eastern.

BASE CITIES

	NO. OF STEWARDES;ES
Miami	941
New York	993
Boston	231
Chicago	166
Atlanta	648
Washington, D.C.	333

An Eastern stewardess's chances of being assigned upon graduation to the base of her choice are usually very good, but not guaranteed. If she does not receive her choice initially, she may transfer at the end of six months if an opening is available.

When trainees graduate from stewardess college, selection of base assignments is determined according to age, with the oldest girl in the class having first choice.

MISCELLANEOUS

Eastern participates in the Thomas Dooley Foundation program.

Opportunities are available for stewardesses to appear in promotional, sales, and other special nonflight assignments, although these are not required. Stewardesses are paid the same rate as their flight pay, based on 2.5 hours per day.

Eastern allows stewardesses to hold outside jobs subject to supervisory approval.

WHERE TO APPLY

Application forms may be obtained by writing to:

Administrator
Stewardess Recruitment
EASTERN AIRLINES A-50
Miami, Florida 33148

Eastern advertises regularly throughout the United States for interviews, and you may apply in person or write to any Eastern employment office. Application is acknowledged within two weeks, and an initial interview is arranged then if a girl meets the general requirements. Following acceptance, the average time before reporting is one month.

National Airlines

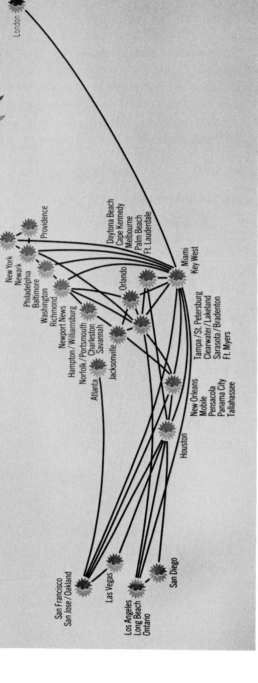

London

Boston
Providence
New York
Newark
Philadelphia
Baltimore
Washington
Richmond
Newport News
Hampton / Williamsburg
Norfolk / Portsmouth
Charleston
Savannah
Atlanta
Jacksonville

Orlando
Daytona Beach
Cape Kennedy
Melbourne
Palm Beach
Ft. Lauderdale
Miami
Key West

Tampa / St. Petersburg
Clearwater / Lakeland
Sarasota / Bradenton
Ft. Myers

New Orleans
Mobile
Pensacola
Panama City
Tallahassee

Houston

San Francisco
San Jose / Oakland
Las Vegas
Los Angeles
Long Beach
Ontario
San Diego

13

NATIONAL AIRLINES

National Airlines employs approximately 1000 stewardesses and has planned no definite rate of expansion. National projects its image as the sun-loving, friendly airline and has been very effective in promoting this image through its stewardesses and advertisements. As an official of a competing airline jokingly complained, "We're more than twice as big as National, but from the way everybody talks you'd think they were bigger."

National services the Eastern Seaboard and has coast-to-coast flights to Florida across the Southwest. They were also recently awarded a route from Florida to London.

Both the headquarters and the training school are in Miami, Florida.

QUALIFICATIONS

Age: 19 to 25.

Height: 5'2" to 5'8".

Weight: 105 to 130 pounds.

Vision: 20/50 minimum uncorrected; contact lenses are permitted.

Marital status: Single or divorced, with no children. Stewardesses who marry during employment may continue flying.

Education: High school plus two years of college or business experience (good working experience is considered particularly desirable).

Language: None required; Spanish helpful.

Citizenship: United States citizen or permanent residence visa.

Health: Must be able to pass National's physical examination.

TRAINING

National's training school is located in Miami. The length of the training period is three and a half weeks, and National pays the cost of room and board. Trainees do not receive a salary during the training period. Observation flights begin the first week of training.

National advises local girls to bring $250 with them to training school, out-of-town girls $450, to cover personal expenses until the first paycheck is received.

UNION

National's stewardesses are affiliated with ALPA; membership is compulsory. There is no initiation fee; dues are $4.50 per month.

UNIFORMS

New graduates pay an initial cost of $280.50 for their first uniform.

A payroll deduction plan is available with installments of $10 per pay period or $20 per month for the basic items, but accessories must be purchased outright by the stewardess.

National pays for all uniform replacements necessitated by wear or a change in design.

Basic items
    3 dresses in vivid orange, lemon, and lime
    1 topcoat
    1 olive-green serving smock
    1 travel carry-all

Accessories
    1 scarf
    2 pair of shoes
    2 pair of gloves
    2 sets of lingerie
    Knee boots (optional)

SALARY

Monthly base pay for 70 hours flown

First six months	$340.00
six months to one year	360.00
Second year	380.00
annual increases to	
Third year	450.00

The minimum number of hours of monthly flight time on National is 70.

Incentive pay rate effective after this minimum is

Jets (per hour)	$9.25

A new stewardess flying 75 hours one month (5 hours' incentive pay) might have a net monthly income of:

Net base pay	$250.00
Net incentive pay	37.25
Expenses	80.00
	$367.25

FRINGE BENEFITS

After six months of service, stewardesses are eligible for paid vacation, which is computed at the rate of 1 1/6 days for each month of active service in the preceding year.

National does not provide educational aid for its stewardesses.

National has a group insurance program for its employees. The stewardess pays 100 percent of the life insurance premium; the company pays 100 percent of the premium for health and hospitalization.

RESERVE POLICY

New stewardesses are on reserve until they have enough seniority to hold a flight. This can be within the first few months of flying.

TRAVEL BENEFITS

Stewardesses are eligible for travel benefits when flying National as soon as they are employed. Initially you receive a 50 percent discount privilege, after six months of service, you pay a $10 service charge per round-trip. These travel benefits are unlimited. Parents receive four trip passes a year; husbands' passes are unlimited. Vacation transportation (one free pass, on National) is furnished for the stewardess and her husband.

National has reduced rate interline agreements with seventy-three airlines.

BASE CITY

National stewardesses have only one base city: Miami.

MISCELLANEOUS

National allows girls to take outside jobs with supervisory approval.

National requires their stewardesses to appear in promotional and nonflight assignments. Girls are paid and credited for scheduled flight hours missed when participating in these special assignments.

14

NORTHEAST AIRLINES

GENERAL INFORMATION

Northeast employs 600 stewardesses and expects to expand the number soon to 1100. Its headquarters and training school are in Boston. Northeast services mainly the Eastern states, but flies as far west as Montreal, Detroit, Chicago, and Cleveland, and as far south as Florida, the Grand Bahamas, and Bermuda.

Since Northeast and Northwest Airlines may merge if the government approves, the information on stewardesses and training for both of these airlines will probably change dramatically. The combined route structures will offer a greater variety, both domestic and international, to their stewardesses.

QUALIFICATIONS

Age: 19½ minimum.

Height: 5'2" to 5'8".

Weight: 105 to 140 pounds, in proportion to height.

Vision: At least 20/50 without glasses or 20/100 in one eye; 20/200 in other eye (minimum) corrected to 20/50 with contact lenses.

Marital status: Single, divorced, or widowed, with no children.

Education: High school graduate; college or business school desirable.

Citizenship: United States citizen or working visa.

Health: Must pass company physical examination.

Miscellaneous: Must be able to swim.

NORTHEAST AIRLINES

TRAINING

Northeast's training school is located in a complex of modern buildings called the Children's Inn in Boston. Quarters are decorated in a bright, cheerful yellow in honor of the Northeast Yellowbirds.

The training period is five weeks. Northeast pays all expenses during training, including lodging and meals, but does not pay a salary during training. The company recommends that you bring about $200 to cover expenses until you receive your first paycheck.

Trainees are housed above the classrooms in the Children's Inn. A cafeteria in the building supplies the food, and the girls have the use of the Inn's swimming pool. There is no strict surveillance of dormitory hours; Northeast feels its girls should be mature enough to observe them without any enforced discipline.

Trainees are sent out on observation flights the first week of training.

After graduation, new stewardesses are allowed five days' hotel expense (no food expenses) until they find an apartment. They must be available to fly forty-eight hours after graduation.

UNION

Northeast's stewardesses are affiliated with ALSSA. Union membership is mandatory after a stewardess's six-month probation period has been completed. The initiation fee is $10, dues $54 per year.

UNIFORMS

The Northeast winter uniform consists of a gold vinyl fit-and-flare coat, pimiento-red jacket, A-line dress, and spice-brown knee-length boots. A new summer uniform is being designed, but details are not yet available.

The cost of the uniform is deducted from your salary at the rate of $6 per paycheck.

Purchased by stewardess (company pays two-thirds of the replacement cost)

2 dresses	$ 85.00	
Jacket	44.50	
All-purpose coat	78.25	
2 scarves	7.90	
Handbag	18.75	
	$234.40	
Gloves (summer)	$ 3.00	
Gloves (winter)	5.95	
Shoes	13.00	(est.)
Serving slippers	5.00	
Panty hose	2.25	
Sunglasses	3.00	
Umbrella *	5.25	
Rain hat *	1.50	
	$ 38.95	
Total cost	$273.35	

Provided by the company
   Boots
   Smock
   Poncho
   Overnight Bag †
   Crests

SALARY

Monthly base pay up to 70 hours' flying time:

First six months	$402.00
Six months to one year	434.00
Second year	461.00
increasing annually to	
Ninth year	658.00

Incentive pay for each hour flown over 70 hours:

Pistons	$7.00
Turbojets	8.00
Jets	9.00

* Optional.
† Returnable.

Expenses: A stewardess receives 45¢ per hour for every hour away from her base, from the time of original departure until the termination of her return flight.

Taxi fare is allowed, not to exceed $2 on any trip from 11 P.M. to 8 A.M., or arrival time 9 P.M. to 6 A.M.

Northeast's stewardesses are paid every Thursday, expense money and incentive pay being included in the last Thursday's paycheck.

A sample weekly paycheck for a new stewardess might be:

Weekly base pay
  minus $18.55 taxes
            6.00 uniform
            1.00 insurance
          $25.55 total deductions
Net weekly base pay $67.21

Monthly incentive pay for a new stewardess flying 78 hours
  might be: $56.00
   minus $11.50 taxes
           $44.50 net
Monthly expenses might be: $80.00
          $124.50 (total expenses and incentive)

The last-of-the-month paycheck would therefore be $191.71 (net weekly base pay plus monthly expenses and incentive pay).

If you add the paychecks together, they will total $393.34 net per month.

FRINGE BENEFITS

After one year of service, Northeast stewardesses are eligible for their first paid vacation of 14 days.

The company offers a complete insurance program, including life, hospitalization, and accident and health insurance. Northeast pays 80 percent of the premium.

Northeast provides educational aid for its stewardesses.

RESERVE POLICY

A new stewardess is on reserve for about eight months until she is senior enough to hold a flight. While on reserve, she is on call five days a week, and has two consecutive days off.

TRAVEL BENEFITS

You are eligible to receive passes on Northeast after six months of employment. These passes are yours for a small service charge, but for the first five years with Northeast they are limited to one a month. Afterward, company passes are unlimited.

Reduced rate privileges become effective after one year of employment.

Parents and husbands share an allotment of three to six passes per year, depending on the stewardess's length of service. Vacation transportation on Northeast is in addition to the regular pass allowance, and is free.

BASE CITIES

	NO. OF STEWARDESSES
Boston	402
New York	100
Miami	150

Northeast estimates that a new stewardess has about a 50 percent chance of being assigned upon graduation to the base of her choice. She may transfer as soon as openings are available.

MISCELLANEOUS

Northeast participates in the Thomas Dooley Foundation program, and offers educational aid.

Stewardesses may hold outside jobs with supervisory approval.

Stewardesses are sometimes asked to appear in promotional and other nonflight assignments. The pay for these special assignments is $5 for less than four hours; $10 for more than four hours, plus all cab fares.

WHERE TO APPLY

Application forms may be obtained by writing to:

NORTHEAST AIRLINES
Stewardess Career Center
500 Boylston Street
Boston, Massachusetts 02116

or from local ticket and airport offices. Personal application may be made at the Boston office, and at other cities serviced by Northeast when interviews are advertised in the local newspapers.

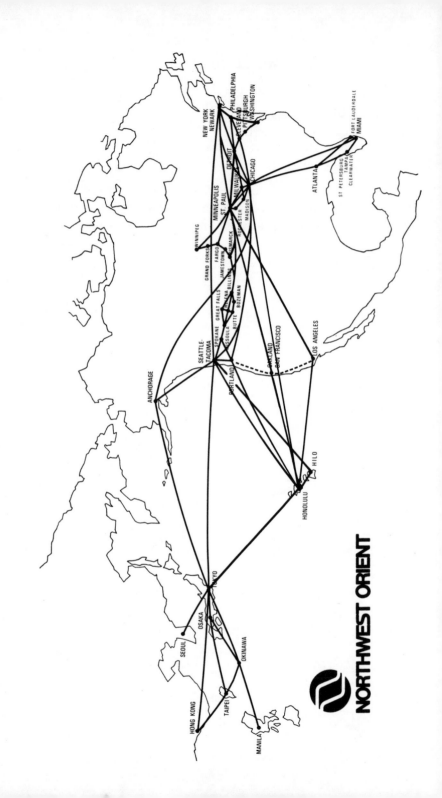

NORTHWEST ORIENT

15

NORTHWEST ORIENT AIRLINES

GENERAL INFORMATION

Northwest Airlines employs about 1800 stewardesses and expects to increase the number to over 3000 by the end of 1970. Their headquarters and training school are in Minneapolis. Northwest is one of the airlines that haven't joined the glamour competition in anything more than inaugurating a fashionable new uniform for their attractive stewardesses. Its training school is in the basement of one of the office and commissary buildings at Minneapolis-St. Paul Airport. Northwest wryly points out that its frugal attitude also makes it one of the few airlines operating in the black.

Though unglamorous, its training facilities are very adequate. Northwest recruits mainly in the Midwest and prefers its stewardesses to be fresh and naturally attractive. Northwest emphasizes service over glamour. If the government allows the merger between Northwest and Northeast, the combined approach should please both farm-fresh and make-up-oriented applicants.

QUALIFICATIONS

Age: 20 minimum.

Height: 5'2" to 5'9".

Weight: 100 to 140 pounds.

Marital status: Unmarried, no children. Stewardesses who marry during employment may continue flying.

Education: High school graduate; college preferred.

Language: No foreign language required.

Citizenship: United States citizen or legal resident.

Health: Must pass physical examination of company.

TRAINING

Northwest Orient's training school is located at Minneapolis-St. Paul Airport; the length of the training period is five weeks. Trainees pay their own room and board while attending school. The company pays each girl a per diem allowance totaling $37 per week while she attends training school. Trainees are advised to bring at least $150 of their own money with them to school to cover personal expenses until the first regular paycheck is received. Trainees begin observation flights the third week of training.

An educational pass to familiarize the stewardesses with their domestic routes on a space-available basis is given after 90 days, and must be used before the end of the six months' probation. This pass may be used only by the stewardess on her own time. It does not have to be used.

International assignments are awarded according to seniority. Northwest estimates that a girl may fly international flights with two years' seniority.

UNION

Northwest Orient's stewardesses are affiliated with ALSSA-TWU; membership is mandatory. Initiation fee is $10; dues are $4.50 per month.

UNIFORMS

Northwest Orient's new look consists of a winter coat in a slightly fitted, princess-line style, in Northwest Orient red, and a visor cap specially designed for Northwest Orient by Yves St.-Laurent. The cap is also in red with a dull black band and a special Northwest Orient logo pin in gold.

A silk scarf features a repeating pattern of the new Northwest Orient logo in red on an off-white background.

An A-line dress and jacket in red, silk-lined gloves, a shoulder bag, luggage, and stretch-leather boots—all in dull black—complete the costume.

1 jacket	$ 47.00
2 dresses	85.00
1 serving smock	9.25
1 hat	22.00
Total	$163.25
1 topcoat	$ 80.00
1 handbag	17.50
1 scarf	4.50
1 pair of gloves	7.50
24-inch suitcase	37.50
Total	$147.00

SALARY

There is no required monthly minimum number of hours of flight time with Northwest Orient. Stewardesses may volunteer for special assignments of a promotional nature; they are paid flight-time credit for this participation.

A probationary period of six months must be completed before a stewardess attains permanent employment status.

The following pay scales became effective June 1, 1968, and a new contract that is now being negotiated will increase the salary.

First six months	$460
Six months to one year	475
Second year	505
Third year	535
Fourth year	550

International assignments are awarded according to seniority.

FRINGE BENEFITS

After one year of service, a stewardess is eligible for two weeks of paid vacation with Northwest Orient. The company has a group life insurance plan and pays 75 percent of the premium;

Northwest also pays 50 percent of the premium for employees' hospitalization insurance.

Northwest des not provide educational aid for its stewardesses.

RESERVE POLICY

New stewardesses are on reserve until they have enough seniority to hold a flight. This can be within the first few months of flying.

TRAVEL BENEFITS

Immediately upon employment, a stewardess is eligible for 75 and 50 percent discount transportation on Northwest Orient's system. After one year of employment she receives two free passes, three passes the second year, etc., up to a limit of seven annual passes. Eligible family members are mother, father, and husband; they can travel on Northwest Orient for a 50 percent discount.

BASE CITIES

	NO. OF STEWARDESSES
Washington, D.C.	35
Minneapolis-St. Paul	1350
Seattle	350

Initially, when a stewardess graduates, she is assigned to Minneapolis-St. Paul. If vacancies and seniority permit, she may request a transfer after six months of service.

MISCELLANEOUS

Northwest Orient participates in the Thomas Dooley Foundation program.

Stewardesses are allowed to take outside jobs with supervisory approval.

WHERE TO APPLY

Application forms may be obtained by writing to:

C. R. Briese
NORTHWEST ORIENT AIRLINES
Personnel Department
Minneapolis-St. Paul Airport
Minneapolis, Minnesota 55111

or from local airport and ticket offices. Application in person may be made at the Minneapolis and Chicago offices. Foreign applications are not solicited, but applicants may write to the Minneapolis office for information.

Upon receipt of a completed application, the company calls the girl in for an interview; acceptance is usually within two weeks of application. Once accepted, a girl can plan on reporting for training in three weeks.

Northwest Orient advertises job opportunities and interviews in newspapers of the large cities along the airline's routes.

16

PAN AMERICAN AIRWAYS

Pan American,* employing 4500 stewardesses, is strictly an international carrier with routes all over the world. Because of this, all Pan Am stewardesses must speak English and at least one other language. Pan Am estimates that about 60 percent of its stewardesses are American and 40 percent foreign. The nationalities of its stewardesses are represented by a corridor of flags at the training school, and each time a girl from a new country graduates from training, there is a ceremony and a new national flag. All of Pan Am's stewardesses are presently based in the United States.

Since Pan Am flies to 119 countries on six continents, the variety of flight assignments is endless for a girl who wants to fly international routes.

For international assignments, Pan Am stewardesses must be able to obtain and maintain a passport, visa, and United States resident status, and be able to travel freely in all countries served by Pan American. Although stewardesses are normally based in the United States, applicants must be willing to accept assignments outside the States should the need arise.

Pan American is seeking girls who have a pleasing personality, poise, tact, and diplomacy, and show a genuine liking for people. It also places great importance on a pleasant speaking voice and good English.

---

* This exclusively international airline quite literally flies all over the world—to 119 countries, to be exact. It has therefore not been possible to provide a Pan Am route map that would fit onto one or even two pages of this book.

QUALIFICATIONS

Age: 20 minimum.

Height: 5'3" to 5'9".

Weight: 105 to 140 pounds, in proportion to height.

Vision: minimum of 20/40 in one eye and no more than 20/100 in the other eye. Contact lenses permitted in special cases.

Marital status: Will consider divorced or widowed with no children. Stewardesses who marry after employment may continue flying.

Education: High school graduate; two years of college preferred.

Language: Must be fluent in English and have a reasonable knowledge of one of the following languages: French, Spanish, Italian, German, Portuguese, Dutch, Swedish, Danish, Norwegian, Finnish, Turkish, Russian, Japanese, Chinese, Arabic, Hindustani, or Greek.

Citizenship: United States citizen or able to obtain an immigration visa to the United States (see Training section for exceptions).

Health: Must be in excellent health and able to pass a flight medical examination. Various innoculations are required.

Miscellaneous: Must be able to swim.

TRAINING

Pan Am has a six-week training program at its stewardess training center in Miami. Girls are housed in a comfortable motel across the street from the training center. The company eventually hopes to build a new stewardess training school to centralize housing and training facilities, but plans have not as yet been completed.

Since Pan Am relies so heavily on foreign girls for language-qualified stewardesses, it has discovered a way of hiring foreign nationals without permanent visas. Trainees are brought into the United States on an H-3 visa (granted for a period of six weeks and called a training visa). The stewardesses then obtain a D-3 visa (called a crewman's visa, which requires the holder to leave the United States every 29 days). Since Pan Am stewardesses always fly out of the country during the month, their visas are automatically renewed when they return.

Pan Am has an intensive cooking course for trainees because it has so many types of first-class service that require these skills. One whole morning is spent teaching the trainees to cook eggs properly. The rest of the training is equally intensive.

For the six-week training period, you are paid a salary of $349.48. Out of this amount, you must pay room and board and incidental expenses. Pan Am advises each girl to bring at least $300 to cover her settling expenses until the first paycheck is received.

There is no policing of the dormitory, as Pan Am feels trainees should be mature enough to observe rules without any surveillance.

UNION

Pan American's stewardesses are affiliated with TWU; membership is compulsory. The initiation fee is $15; dues are $4 per month.

UNIFORMS

The Pan American uniform consists of two outfits—a gold jumper and a blue camisole-top skirt, each with matching jacket—plus blue greatcoat tailored in a version of the classic Chesterfield. A bowler hat is worn with the coat. Accessories such as shoes, boots, gloves, handbag, and silk scarf are honey-brown. The in-flight serving smock is a French butcher's apron.

1 overcoat (blue)	$ 81.64
1 jacket (blue)	55.64
1 jacket (gold)	55.64
1 skirt (blue)	29.64
1 jumper (gold)	42.64
4 blouses	37.00
2 hats	28.00
2 aprons	9.84
1 handbag	13.88
1 overnight bag	6.02
Total	$359.94

Uniform cost is deducted at the rate of $16 per paycheck. Uniform replacements are made by Pan American.

SALARY

Monthly base pay for 67 hours' flight time:

First six months	$478.63
Six months to one year	526.26
Second year	586.60
increasing to	
Third year	665.96

Incentive pay for each hour flown over 67:

First six months	$ 10.26
Six months to one year	11.28
Second year	12.57
increasing to	
Third year	14.27

Stewardesses are eligible for the job of purser after a probationary period of six months, when there are openings.

With promotion to purser, it is possible to earn upwards of $10,000 a year within three years from the date of initial employment. However, a new stewardess flying 70 hours (13 hours' incentive pay) might have a *net* monthly income of:

Base pay	$382.90	(taxes and uniform deducted)
Incentive pay	105.80	(taxes deducted)
Expenses *	120.00	
	$608.70	

Pan American stewardesses fly an average of 80 hours a month.

FRINGE BENEFITS

After one year of employment, Pan Am stewardesses are eligible for 30 days of paid vacation per year. During the first

---

* Expense money is given to each stewardess at her layover stops in the currency of the country she is in.

year of employment, vacation is accrued at the rate of 2½ days per month of service, which may be taken after January 1.

Pan American has a complete insurance program with the company paying hospitalization insurance and most of the premium on the group life policy.

Pan American does not have an educational aid program, but does have language laboratories which it hopes will encourage its stewardesses to learn additional languages.

RESERVE POLICY

Pan Am has a rotating reserve policy which assures new stewardesses of holding a bid the majority of the time.

TRAVEL BENEFITS

After 90 days of employment a stewardess is eligible to receive unlimited reduced-fare benefits on Pan Am as well as on most other airlines. These range from 50 percent positive-space discounts to 75 percent space-available. Once a year, during vacation, the stewardess and members of her immediate family may fly anywhere served by Pan Am, at a 90 percent discount.

BASE CITIES

	NO. OF STEWARDESSES
New York	1328
Miami	514
San Francisco	920
Seattle	103
Washington, D.C.	139
Chicago	103
Hawaii	122
Los Angeles	309

Pan American will assist a stewardess arriving at a new base in arranging temporary hotel reservations, and will provide her with information concerning apartment vacancies.

New graduates draw lots to determine seniority when bidding for available base assignments. After completion of the six-month probationary period, a girl may request a transfer to the base of her choice. Thereafter, she must remain at a base for at least one year.

MISCELLANEOUS

Pan American participates in the Thomas Dooley Foundation program.

Outside jobs are allowed by the company with supervisory approval.

Promotional and nonflight special assignments are available if a stewardess wishes to participate. Girls are paid for these special assignments.

WHERE TO APPLY

Miss Anne Adams, Flight Service Recruiting
PAN AMERICAN WORLD AIRWAYS
Hangar 14, JFK International Airport
Jamaica, New York 11430

Or, Pan Am employment offices at International Airport, San Francisco, California 94128; or PAA Building, N.W. 37th Street, Miami, Florida 33159. Personal applications may also be made at these offices any weekday morning. Girls who live outside the United States should communicate with the New York Pan Am office, above, and ask when an interviewer will be in their area.

Travel and the other personal expenses of being interviewed are paid by the applicant.

Upon the airline's receipt of a completed application, every girl who meets the basic requirements is called for her first personal interview. After this initial interview, you are notified from the New York office if you are to be invited back for a final interview. Girls who have not heard from New York one week following their first interview can assume they have not been accepted.

Once accepted, you should plan to report for training no later than one month from acceptance—perhaps immediately, if you are available for work.

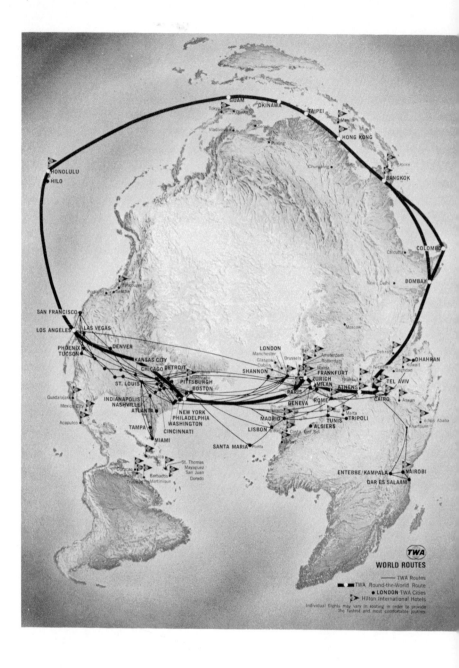

17

TRANS WORLD AIRLINES

Trans World Airlines has around-the-world routes as well as a large domestic operation servicing most of the United States. Its hostesses (it prefers this term) are divided into two groups: domestic and international. Although the international division has two foreign bases open only to foreign nationals and subject to a different working agreement, the majority of the international hostesses are hired and based in the United States.

Those based in New York fly to Western Europe and Tel Aviv; those based on the West Coast fly military charters to Southeast Asia and commercial flights as far as Hong Kong.

Because hostesses can transfer back and forth between the domestic and international divisions, TWA offers the most variety geographically to any potential hostess who may not know what routes she would enjoy working.

QUALIFICATIONS

Age: 19½ minimum.

Height: 5'2" to 5'9".

Weight: 100 to 140 pounds, in proportion to height.

Vision: 20/200 is the minimum acceptable, if correctable to 20/30. Contact lenses are permitted if the applicant has been wearing them successfully prior to acceptance. Eyeglasses are permitted.

Marital status: TWA hires single, divorced, and married women who are willing to accept any base assignment for the first six months.

Education: High school graduate.

Language: Domestic stewardesses: English required; foreign languages desirable. International: In order to qualify for trans-atlantic service, a girl must be able to speak and understand the language of one country into which TWA operates. Fluency in German, Spanish, French, Greek, Italian, or other languages spoken in Europe would fulfill this requirement.

Citizenship: United States citizen or permanent entry visa.

Health: Must be able to pass TWA's physical examination.

TRAINING

TWA has recently opened a multi-million-dollar hostess training college which offers all the latest training equipment, and, of course, luxuries. Located outside Kansas City, Breech Training Academy claims to be the most advanced in the world.

The training period lasts five weeks, followed by a week of additional training at the hostess's assigned base.

Trainees must live in the college dormitory, where their rooms cost them $15.00 per week. TWA begins paying hostesses from the first day of training, at the rate of $245 a month. The first of these checks does not come for two weeks, so each girl is advised to bring an additional $100 with her to meet expenses.

UNION

TWA's hostesses are affiliated with ALSSA; membership is compulsory. The initiation fee is $10; dues are $4.50 per month.

UNIFORMS

TWA hostesses wear wool knit dresses and jackets in poppy red, green, or yellow with poppy-red accessories and a poppy-red all-weather coat. The choice of dress color is up to the hostess.

In the summer, a washable white-topped, plaid-skirted dress with a blazer of navy blue, green, or brown is worn with white accessories and a navy raincoat. The plaid skirt of the dress is made up of the colors of the blazers.

Uniforms are paid for by the hostess at the rate of $16 per

month, deducted biweekly from each paycheck. After the initial uniforms are paid for, TWA provides all replacements necessitated by wear or a change in design.

SALARY

Domestic

Monthly base pay for 68 hours' flight time:

First six months	$376.00
Six months to one year	396.00
Second year	424.00
Annual increases to	
Seventh year	580.00

Incentive pay for each hour flown over 68:

First six months	$ 6.36
Six months to one year	6.70
One year	7.17
Annual increases to	
Seven years	9.81

International

Base pay for 65 hours' flight time:

First six months	$424.00
Six months to one year	444.00
Second year	472.00
Annual increases to	
Seven years	596.00

Incentive pay for each hour flown over 65:

First six months	$ 7.19
Six months to one year	7.59
Second year	7.99
Annual increases to	
Seven years	10.08

Expenses: Domestic expenses are computed at 45¢ per hour from the time of leaving on flight to time of return. International expenses are from 45¢ per hour up to 50¢, depending on the city of layover, and are computed only from time of arrival to time of departure from layover station, since meals are provided on the airplane.

Taxi fares are provided during certain hours for domestic flights and for every trip on international.

Paychecks are received every two weeks; expenses and incentive pay on the 25th of every month. A sample net monthly income for a new hostess on domestic routes, flying 73 hours a month (5 hours' incentive pay) might be:

Net monthly base pay	$293.00 (taxes & uniform deducted)
Net incentive pay	25.30
Expenses	70.00
	$388.30

Girls who are assigned directly to the international division make about $75 more per month.

This salary will soon change; a new contract is being negotiated which should result in an increase in both base and incentive pay.

FRINGE BENEFITS

During the first seven years of employment, a hostess based in the continental United States is eligible for 15 days of paid vacation. You become eligible for a vacation on January of each year, provided you have completed the six-month probationary period. Vacation time is not cumulative, and must be taken within the calendar year.

TWA has a complete insurance program including group life, hospitalization, and accident and health insurance. The company pays all the premiums on the latter.

At the major hostess bases, TWA provides language laboratories consisting of records, tape recordings, and individual instruction to assist those who would like to learn or refresh their knowledge of French, German, Italian, or Spanish.

TWA offers educational aid to its hostesses.

RESERVE POLICY

New stewardesses are on reserve until they have enough seniority to hold a flight. This can be within the first few months on domestic, but is likely to be longer on international.

TRAVEL BENEFITS

After six months of employment, a hostess is eligible to receive two domestic passes on TWA, including vacation transportation; four domestic passes after one year. After three years, passes may be used on international routes. Pass privileges increase with seniority. Parents and husbands are eligible for TWA passes, subject to the same conditions and paying a small service charge.

TWA has interline reduced-rate transportation agreements with the majority of United States airlines, and with some international lines. There are also reciprocal pass agreements with other United States airlines.

BASE CITIES

	NO. OF STEWARDESSES
New York (domestic	700
and international)	850
Newark (domestic)	200
Boston (domestic)	300
Chicago (domestic)	600
Kansas City, Mo. (domestic)	700
Los Angeles (domestic	850
and international)	300
San Francisco (domestic	600
and international)	100

MISCELLANEOUS

TWA participates in the Thomas Dooley Foundation program. Outside jobs are allowed, with supervisory approval.

Hostesses are requested (not required) to appear in promotional and nonflight special assignments. Hostesses are credited with 2.8 hours of flight pay, except when received from a flight for these purposes, in which case they receive pay and credit for trips missed on a scheduled basis.

WHERE TO APPLY

Manager, Flight Crew Employment
TRANS WORLD AIRLINES
10 Richards Road
Kansas City, Missouri 64108

Personal interviews are conducted in major American cities. TWA advertises interviews and employment opportunities on the Sunday preceding the scheduled interview in a particular city. Check the Sunday classified advertisement section or general news section of the local paper if you live in or near a major city serviced by TWA.

18

UNITED AIR LINES

United Air Lines employs approximately 5500 stewardesses and expects to increase the number to 8,000 by 1975. One of the largest United States airlines, United services most of America, Vancouver, B.C., and was one of the first airlines servicing Hawaii.

United's headquarters are in Chicago, where they have constructed a multimillion-dollar stewardess training center in Elk Grove, bordering the airport. United was one of the first airlines to initiate more effective emergency training methods for stewardesses, many of which have been adopted by other major airlines.

United considers college or registered-nurse training very desirable, and this would be a plus factor for an applicant. But girls who do not meet *all* basic qualifications will not be considered.

QUALIFICATIONS

Age: 20 minimum, although girls will be considered at 19½ and can be accepted for future training. United requires that girls sign an agreement upon employment that they will retire at 32.

Height: 5'2" to 5'9".

Weight: 105 to 140 pounds, in proportion to height.

Vision: Must be correctable to 20/30 in each eye. If vision is 20/50 or worse, the stewardess must wear contact lenses or eyeglasses.

Marital status: Single. Once employed, stewardesses who marry may continue flying.

Education: High school diploma.

Language: English (United is strictly domestic).

Citizenship: United States citizen or permanent visa.

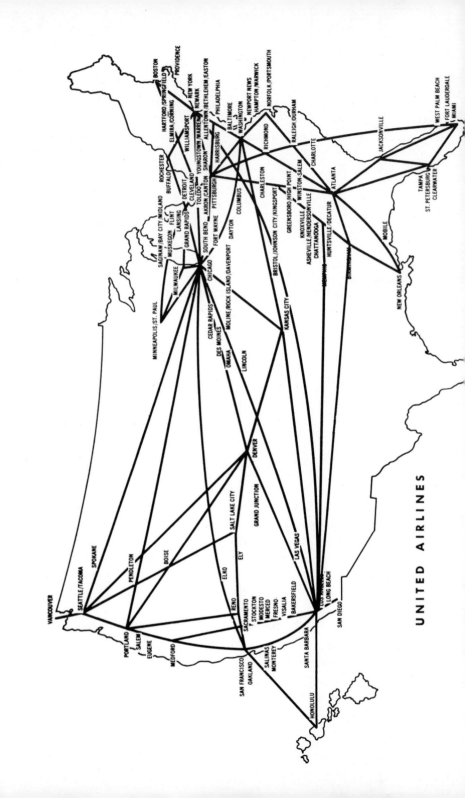

UNITED AIRLINES

TRAINING

United's training school is a very well equipped center in Elk Grove, Illinois, that provides housing, meals, and luxuries, such as a heated swimming pool and tennis courts. The training period is five and one-half weeks long, and no salary is paid during that time. United suggests that each girl bring $400 with her, to cover incidental and settling expenses until her first paycheck is received.

United's training program is run by a very competent staff utilizing education and visual aids. Most of the excellent instruction in service and emergency training is by demonstration and performance in the mock-ups, with a minimum of lectures.

UNION

United's stewardesses are affiliated with ALPA; membership is voluntary. Dues are $4.50 per month.

UNIFORMS

The main component of United's uniform is three basic wool dresses, in varying color combinations. Each girl has two dresses, coral red and bright navy, both with contrasting creamy banding. She then has the choice of a third dress in cream with the option of blue or red banding.

The winter coat and "kepi" hat are coral red.

The summer raincoat is cream with contrasting hat.

Accessories include a blue handbag, square-toed calfskin shoes, white gloves, red luggage, navy knee-high boots.

The cost of the uniform is $375, and is deducted from paychecks at the rate of $35 per month.

United is in the process of changing its uniform design, but the cost will be approximately the same.

SALARY

Monthly base pay for up to 70 hours' flying time:

First six months	$455
Six months to one year	470

Second year	485
annual increases to:	
Ninth year	660

Incentive pay for each hour flown over 70:
$11 per flight hour

Expenses:

Breakfast	$1.75
Lunch	2.00
Dinner	4.35
Midnight snack	1.50

Taxi fare when flight departure is between 10 P.M. and 8 A.M. and when arrival time is between 8 P.M. and 10 A.M. is allowed at the rate of $2.25.

An average monthly net income for a new stewardess flying 75 hours (5 hours' incentive pay) might be:

Net base pay	$329	(taxes and uniform
Net incentive pay	50	deducted)
Expenses	100	
	$479	

FRINGE BENEFITS

You are eligible for your first vacation during the second calendar year of employment. Annual paid vacation time is 16 days after one full calendar year of service.

United has a complete insurance program, including group life, hospitalization, and accident and health; the company pays all premiums.

United does not offer educational aid to its stewardesses.

RESERVE POLICY

United has a rotating reserve policy throughout its seniority list, which assures junior hostesses of holding a bid the majority of the time.

TRAVEL BENEFITS

Immediately upon employment, you are eligible for unlimited reduced rates on United at a 50 percent discount. After one year of service, you are allowed four passes. Parents share in these travel benefits.

BASE CITIES

	NO. OF STEWARDESSES
New York	540
Newark	350
Chicago	1200
Washington, D.C.	350
Miami	250
Los Angeles	950
San Francisco	400
Denver	300
Honolulu	150
MAC operations	50

MISCELLANEOUS

United Air Lines participates in the Thomas Dooley Foundation program.

United does not require its stewardesses to appear in promotional or nonflight assignments, but this sort of work is available. The pay for these special assignments is $2 per hour.

Stewardesses are permitted to take outside jobs with supervisory approval.

WHERE TO APPLY

United prefers that applicants write to personnel offices requesting application forms. If you fulfill the basic eligibility requirements, a personal interview will be arranged.

United advertises interviews and employment opportunities in the local newspapers of cities serviced by the airline.

Some of the personnel offices are:

UNITED AIR LINES
Hangar No. 8
Kennedy International Airport
Jamaica, New York 11430

UNITED AIR LINES
O'Hare Field
Box 66140
Chicago, Illinois 60666

UNITED AIR LINES
Stapleton Airfield
Denver, Colorado 80207

UNITED AIR LINES
6000 Avion Drive
Los Angeles, California 90009

UNITED AIR LINES
Seattle-Tacoma International Airport
Seattle, Washington 98158

19

WESTERN AIRLINES INTERNATIONAL

Western employs over 1000 stewardesses and expects to increase the number to 8000 by the end of 1975. From these figures you can see that Western has big plans for expansion. Western's headquarters and training school are in Los Angeles. It services the Western states and seaboard as far north as Alaska and as far south as Mexico. It flies inland as far as Minneapolis, but with its new routes to Hawaii, Western's is mainly a sun-drenched image even though some of it comes from the northern midnight sun.

Western is the only major airline that works directly with private training schools for stewardesses. Many of its successful applicants come from the California State Junior College system, with whom Western has coordinated courses, even providing old equipment such as mock-ups. This does not mean these girls are assured of being hired or can skip Western's five-week training program, but it does give recruiters a choice of well-prepared applicants.

QUALIFICATIONS

Age: 20 minimum.

Height: 5'2"to 5'9".

Weight: 100 to 140 pounds, in proportion to height.

Vision: Minimum acceptable is 20/50 in both eyes. Contact lenses are acceptable if applicant has been wearing them successfully prior to acceptance.

Marital status: Single, widowed, or divorced, with no children. Stewardesses who marry during employment may continue flying.

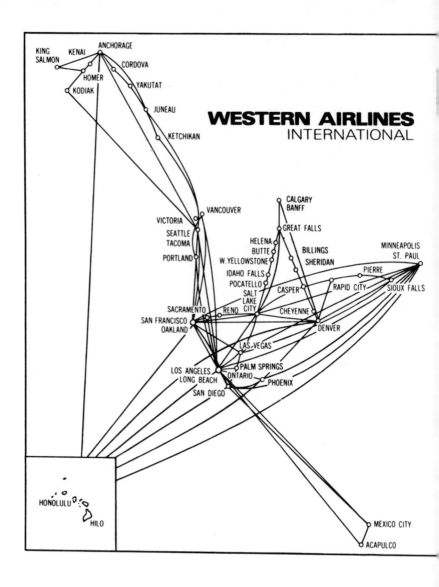

WESTERN AIRLINES
INTERNATIONAL

Education: High school graduate or better.

Language: English; conversational Spanish required for Mexican flights.

Citizenship: United States citizen, or, if foreign, permanent working visa.

Health: Must pass Western's physical examination.

TRAINING

Western's well-equipped training school is located at Los Angeles Airport, and the trainees are housed in a nearby hotel (local girls may live at home). Training lasts five weeks. At the end of training, girls are paid a total of $350, out of which they must pay hotel bills and meals—hotel expenses are approximately $25 per week. During training two advances of $50 each are allowed out of the $350. Western suggests each girl bring $300 with her to cover personal settling expenses until her first paycheck, since most of the salary paid at the end of training will be used up by room and board and by uniform items.

Western also pays three days' hotel expenses to new graduates while they find apartments.

Western has a unique graduation ceremony at the end of training. It flies the whole class to one of the cities on its routes, and prominent businessmen in the community take an active part in the ceremony. Each graduate is sponsored by one of these businessmen, who pins on her wings and then escorts her to a deluxe luncheon. Western says that many lasting friendships are formed between the businessmen and their "airline stepdaughters."

UNION

Western stewardesses are affiliated with ALPA; membership is compulsory. There is no initiation fee; dues are $4.50 per month.

UNIFORMS

The basic uniform costs the stewardess approximately $200.

This may be paid through payroll deduction at the rate of $12.50 per paycheck. Western will provide all replacements.

The Western uniform consists of two dresses, one red and one navy blue, a full-length coat in navy blue, scarlet waistcoat and hat. Navy-blue boots and shoes, gloves, and a tote bag accessorize the outfit.

The summer uniform uses the same dress with lightweight accessories, including a raincoat and scarf. Aluminum overnight luggage, a flight bag, and a garment bag are provided with the wardrobe.

SALARY

A new contract is being negotiated which will increase the salary scale. The present scale is:

Monthly base pay for up to 67 hours' flight time:

First six months	$350.00
Six months to one year	395.00
Second year	410.00
annual increase to	
Eighth year	520.00

International flight pay (Mexico):

Add per round-trip	$ 4.00

Incentive pay for each hour flown over 67:

Turbine per hour	$ 8.00
Piston per hour	6.00

Stewardesses are allowed to fly a maximum of only 80 hours a month.

A stewardess's expense allowance while engaged in flight operations away from her base station is 40¢ per hour.

Taxi fare for flights leaving between 6 P.M. and 8 A.M., or arriving between 8 P.M. and 7 A.M. is $1.75.

Stewardesses are paid on the 5th and 20th of every month. Expenses and incentive pay are received on the 20th.

A sample paycheck for the 5th of the month for a new

stewardess, flying 75 hours (8 hours of the 75 are for incentive pay, piston) might be:

Base pay	$175.00	
minus		$35.00 taxes
		12.50 uniform
		3.50 insurance
		$51.00
Net base pay		$124.00

The 20th-of-the-month paycheck would be the same net base pay:

		$124.00
plus 8 hrs. incentive pay (piston)	$48.00	
minus	9.60 taxes	
Net incentive pay		39.40
Plus expenses		80.00
Total		$243.40

FRINGE BENEFITS

Western's stewardesses accrue vacation time after one month of flying. From one to five years' service, you receive 14 days' paid vacation.

Western offers group life insurance, hospitalization and accident and health insurance, for a premium of $5 per month to California residents, and $7.75 per month to non-Californians.

RESERVE POLICY

New stewardesses are on reserve until they have enough seniority to hold a flight. This can be within the first few months of flying.

TRAVEL BENEFITS

After completing her first six months of service, a stewardess is eligible to begin receiving travel benefits on Western. Eligible family members—parents, husbands, and stepchildren—may receive courtesy passes on an annual allotment based on the stewardess's length of service as follows:

Six months to 1 year	2 passes
Second year	4 passes
Third year and after	6 passes

A stewardess may designate any portion of her allotment for use by members of her immediate family.

Unlimited 50 percent positive-space transportation on Western's entire system, including Mexico and Canada, is available from the date of employment on.

BASE CITIES

	NO. OF STEWARDESSES
Los Angeles	475
San Francisco	222
Seattle	110
Salt Lake City	130
Denver	132
Minneapolis	60

A stewardess graduating from training school has a good chance of being assigned to the base of her choice. After six months of employment she may request a change of base assignment.

New graduates are awarded their base assignments on a bid basis established by class seniority, determined by age.

MISCELLANEOUS

Western participates in the Thomas Dooley Foundation program.

Although Western does not encourage outside work, it is allowed with supervisory approval. However, the company prefers each girl to devote her off-duty hours to activities which will provide her with the rest and relaxation necessary to prepare her for the next work assignment.

WHERE TO APPLY

WESTERN AIRLINES
International Airport
Avion Building
6060 Avion Drive
Los Angeles, California 9009

Application may also be made through regional stewardess managers of any of Western's base cities, or from the station manager of any city served by Western. Application forms are available at local ticket offices and all airport offices.

If a girl living outside the United States wants to apply, she should first obtain a permanent working visa.

Once a completed application has been received, a form letter is sent calling the applicant in for an appointment. Western provides free transportation to Los Angeles from any point in its system for final testing and interview. Acceptance is usually within a week. The applicant will be informed for which new class she is being considered; classes are usually held at six- to seven-week intervals.

20
OTHER AIRLINES

There are additional airlines in the United States—small regional and trunk airlines, and charter airlines. For information on qualifications, salary, etc., there is a handbook published yearly by the International Stewardess News—a newspaper that gives monthly reports on new uniforms, new contracts, and all news pertinent to airline stewardesses all over the world. Copies of the *Annual Guide to Careers As an Airline Stewardess* may be obtained from:

360 East First Avenue
Hialeah, Florida 33010

GLOSSARY

American Flag Carrier: Any airline registered in the United States.

Bid: A schedule of flight sequences over a period of a month which gives you your flight number, layover stops, flight time, flight dates, and time off.

Cabin crew: The stewardesses.

Cock-pit crew: The Captain, First Officer, and Flight Engineer. On long flights the cock-pit crew includes a Second Officer.

Deadhead: Any crew member who is flying as a passenger returning from or going to a flight assignment.

Expense check: Each airline pays its stewardesses' expenses while they are out on trips. This money usually is paid the month after the expenses are incurred.

Galley: The part of the airplane where food is prepared and stored.

Holding a bid: A stewardess assigned a flight sequence is "holding a bid." "Bids" are awarded by seniority—that is, the most senior girl has first choice, other girls' choices being determined by their number on the seniority list.

Incentive pay: Stewardesses are paid a base salary for a certain specified number of flight hours per month. For each hour flown above that amount, they receive incentive pay. Flying many hours of overtime can increase your salary considerably. Seniority increases your chances of "holding bids" with high flight times.

Junior girl: A new stewardess; also, any stewardess on the bottom half of the seniority list.

Layover: Any city on your airline's routes in which you are given "legal rest"—which means that after flying a certain number of hours you are allowed a certain number of hours' rest. Often layovers are longer than the legal rest coming to you, allowing you an enjoyable interlude in a city you may like.

MAC PAC: Military Air Charter; a charter flight which carries military personnel.

Mechanical: Any delay in your flight which is due to a mechanical failure of the aircraft.

Open flights: Flights without sufficient crew members. Stewardesses may trade into them; failing that, Scheduling will assign a reserve girl to the flight.

Pass: An airline ticket, available to airline personnel and their families for a small service charge, which allows them to travel "space available."

Piston: Propeller aircraft, as opposed to jets which have no propellers.

Positive space: Guarantees you a seat on a flight, just as if you were a full-fare passenger.

Reduced rates: Airlines have agreements with each other allowing airline personnel to buy tickets at reduced rates. In the United States, the reduction is 50 percent, assuring "positive space." International tickets may be bought at a reduction of 75 percent for "space available" and 50 percent for "positive space."

Reserve: Also known as "the pool," or "stand-by." There are always more stewardesses at a base than there are bids available. Those too junior to "hold a bid" are put on reserve and assigned to flights when the regular stewardesses are sick. They may also be assigned to charter flights.

Rotating reserve: Some airlines rotate reserve duty among all the stewardesses instead of leaving it for the junior stewardesses. This means that every girl is on reserve perhaps once or twice a year.

Scheduling: The office that assigns "bids" and "open flights." This office organizes the schedules and makes sure every flight is supplied with its proper compliment of crew members.

Senior girl: A stewardess who has been working long enough to be on the upper half of the seniority list; the benefits being senior flights (high flying time, good layovers and time off) and the assurance of holding a flight schedule which suits her (holidays and weekends off if desired).

Space available: A literal term: if there is room on the flight after all the paying passengers have boarded, "pass" holders are given those empty seats.

Stewardess: Also known by the terms "hostess," "cabin attendant," "flight attendant," "cabin crew member."

Turnaround: A flight sequence which takes you out to a city and straight back to your home base, sometimes in the same day.

Weight check: As unwelcome as an "expense check" is welcome. Stewardesses who weigh more than the amount specified by the airline for their height are put on "weight check." This can mean your being weighed before every flight until you lose the offending pounds. If you don't succeed within the time allowed, you may be taken off schedule until you do.